Christmas 20

Merry Cdr

from Larry & Betty

THE DOVER-PHILA FOOTBALL RIVALRY

THE DOVER-PHILA FOOTBALL RIVALRY

A TRADITION SHARED THROUGH ITS GREATEST GAMES

MATTHEW S. LAUTZENHEISER
FOREWORDS BY WARD HOLDSWORTH AND TOM ARMSTRONG

Charleston · London
The History Press

Published by The History Press
Charleston, SC 29403
www.historypress.net

Copyright © 2011 by Matthew S. Lautzenheiser

All rights reserved

First published 2011

Manufactured in the United States

ISBN 978.1.59629.991.7

Library of Congress CIP data applied for.

Notice: The information in this book is true and complete to the best of our knowledge. It is offered without guarantee on the part of the author or The History Press. The author and The History Press disclaim all liability in connection with the use of this book.

All rights reserved. No part of this book may be reproduced or transmitted in any form whatsoever without prior written permission from the publisher except in the case of brief quotations embodied in critical articles and reviews.

Para Kelly, siempre

Contents

Forewords, by Ward Holdsworth and Tom Armstrong	9
Acknowledgements	13
Introduction	15
1. The Early Years: 1896–1929	19
2. Two Decades of Outstanding Players: 1930–1949	45
3. An Era of Change: 1950–1969	69
4. The Cardinal Conference Years: 1970–1989	99
5. The Modern Era: 1990–2010	127
Conclusion	151
Dover-Phila Rivalry Timeline	155
About the Author	159

FOREWORDS

Visitors to the Dover–New Philadelphia area might reflect on its beauty, thinking, "You can't tell where one community ends and the other begins." That may be true. However, those who live here have no doubt about whether they live in Dover or New Philadelphia. These folks live together, work together and are related to one another. But when it comes to the week of the Dover-Phila football game, everyone knows exactly where you live and whose side you are on. You may be a Dover graduate living in Phila, or vice versa, but that doesn't matter. What matters is where you went to school or where your kids or grandkids are in school right now. For some diehards, they won't even consider living in the other community, even though their work may be there. And so it goes.

Otherwise normal people have a common dislike for one another concerning the outcome of a football game. And why is this game so important? The answers may vary. The reality is that it's definitely important.

And how fierce is this rivalry? Would you believe that after one hundred years, the resulting outcomes were exactly even? Of course, there were stretches of time when the outcomes favored one team over the other. But we all know nothing lasts forever. Just wait until next year!

So why make a history of such a thing? Well, why do we keep records? Why do we have reunions or publish yearbooks? To conjure up memories, I guess, so we can "go home again." Probably each of us has our own special memories of a particular time or game in this long

Forewords

series. I remember my father-in-law's favorite: when the Miskimen boy kicked the field goal to win the game for Phila in 1946. I asked Hugh Miskimen one time, "Are you the one who kicked the field goal to win the Dover game?"

"No!" he said. "That was my brother. But I can tell you exactly where he kicked it from and where I was standing when he did it!" Memories.

I was fortunate enough to have played, coached in and, like many others, witnessed countless numbers of these contests. When I think of those games, the same vividness I held then returns. I'm sure that when you read Matt's accounts of those thrilling days of yesteryear, the same will happen to you. Then, as recorded in my 1957 *Delphian* yearbook, "conversation will stop for an instant as a memory threads its way among your thoughts. Then, it is lost, and only the afterglow of hard work and good times remains as a pleasant, well-remembered period of your life."

Thanks to Matt's efforts, we can all go home again through the medium of memory. Let us cherish these past accounts of this great rivalry as we recall special times in our lives.

Ward Holdsworth
NPHS Class of 1957

I saw my first Dover versus Phila football game in 1951. My father was coaching with "Dutch" Furbay. I was twelve years old and in the seventh grade. Dover lost that year, but I surely understood the significance of that game, and I loved being a part of it.

By my junior year in high school, New Philadelphia had put together a string of six wins and one tie. Dover had not won for seven years.

In 1955, we beat the rival Quakers soundly, but it didn't last. They won the next few, but then things began to change.

The memories and dreams conjured up about this traditional rivalry are strong and long-lasting. I am pretty sure the dreams of the young boys who play in this long rivalry draw up images of brutal fights in the trenches and heroic game-winning plays.

For the old-timers, those visions are real, and many of us can remember and talk about specific plays, strange occurrences, spots on the playing field

Forewords

where great plays were made, who played across from us and "the thrill of victory and the agony of defeat."

When you read through the record books, you can almost see the pendulum swinging, along with the names of players from the two towns.

When "Doc" Kelker was in Dover, or "Bronco" Reese was attending New Philadelphia, you could view the fortunes of the football clubs changing during those years.

When Matt first approached me to write this foreword, I was pleased and honored. Matt had been a student of mine, he played running back at Dover and we attended the same church. He was, and still is, a fine young man of high standards, with a strong work ethic, and is a credit to our communities. Without a doubt, Matt has been influenced by his experiences taken from this storied rivalry and the great game of football.

Traditions, both at the schools and in the communities, have become such a strong part of this annual game, and Matt has done a beautiful job of capturing them here.

I was pleased to learn that my counterpart, penning the foreword from the New Philadelphia perspective, is Ward Holdsworth, with whom I maintain a wonderful friendship. Ward and I played against each other in high school and college and then coached against each other. To this day, we remain friends and still hold to our philosophy of coaching: teaching the young men who played for us about football, but more importantly, using that experience to teach lessons about discipline, respect, hard work, courage, team work and responsibility—lessons they will hopefully carry with them throughout their lives.

This year, I am excited to watch my grandson become a fourth-generation member of Dover football. My father, Tom Sr., coached in the 1950s, '60s and '70s and began a tradition of writing a poem for the annual Dover–New Philadelphia Pep Rally. Some may recall the "Battle of the Bat" being one of his first. After his retirement, I inherited the task, but not being the poet he was, I struggled. But it became an enjoyable part of my coaching. I always tried to touch on the importance of tradition, the glory of the game and those who participated before us. Parents, classmates, bands and cheerleaders are all an integral part of this big game.

I have included excerpts from several of the poems my father and I wrote during our fifty-odd years of coaching:

FOREWORDS

Past glories surround us, be strong you young lads
 You've got all the support of grandfathers and dads,
Neighbors, and uncles and men never known
 Tonight you young warriors make memories of your own.

The grass on the gridiron is trampled and red
 With the blood of the victorious team.
Battered and bruised, with a smile on their face
 Stands a well-oiled and fine-tuned machine.

From way in the back of your mind somewhere
 The memories come rushing today,
Of a few little boys in a backyard game
 And now there's just one left to play.
Those memories flood o'er us, they come in a flash,
 A last second catch for a score
A game saving tackle, a fight in the trenches
 Fond memories, tonight there'll be more.
But memories and dreams don't belong to just you.
 They belong to a parent, a friend.
They belong to past warriors of the Crimson and Gray.
 What nostalgia, those memories won't end.

Things change, time moves on and who knows the future. But for now, let us hope it will continue.

Matt has done a magnificent job putting together a historical overview of this great game that holds two small Ohio communities together. Enjoy the book and the memories.

Tom Armstrong
Dover Coach

Acknowledgements

As with any project of this scope, this book would not have been possible without the assistance of many individuals. This project began nearly two years ago when I was contacted by Dover native and editor for The History Press Joe Gartrell. For several years, Joe had kicked around the idea of doing a project focusing on the Dover-Phila rivalry. Working with local history projects every day, Joe understood the potential of such a project and began to look for authors. Having done a book on Dover's history in 2009, and as head of the Dover Historical Society and J.E. Reeves Home, I was on his list. From the time I first spoke with Joe, I was interested in working with him on the book. It was a great opportunity, and I owe a great debt to Joe for giving me the chance to work on this project.

Once the book was underway, I quickly realized how involved the research would be. In this department, I benefitted incredibly from the efforts of Fred Miller and the Tuscarawas County Historical Society. Fred has been a huge help in this process, both as a sounding board and as a researcher. Without the countless hours Fred and his staff put in, this book would have been ready for the 2015 rivalry game instead of the 2011 game.

In addition to Fred Miller and the Tuscarawas County Historical Society, I was also very fortunate to get to know Dover High School biographer Denny Rubright. Denny has self-published nine books on Dover's football history, and I'm convinced he has forgotten more about football then I will ever know. Through the course of researching his books, Denny also uncovered

Acknowledgements

a great deal of New Phila football history. Throughout the process, Denny has provided encouragement, read through drafts and provided countless sources and tidbits of information. Dover is lucky to have Denny and has benefited greatly from his lifelong passion for high school football.

In addition to those above, many others acted as readers or contributed pictures. Among these are Duke Strickmaker, Dave Contini, Fred and Carolyn Delphia, Terry Edwards at Mitchell's Studio, the Quaker Foundation and the Dover Historical Society. Many readers helped to shape the text, including Dover athletic director Kevin Keffer, New Phila athletic director Tom Farbizo and Larry Lautzenheiser.

In addition to all the help provided by these great individuals, this book received the proverbial icing on the cake when New Philadelphia's Ward Holdsworth and Dover's Tom Armstrong agreed to write forewords. I can't imagine two better individuals who understand the rivalry and, more importantly, what it means to their respective communities.

As a boy growing up in Dover, I was interested in football in the same way that many other young men have been over the years, but my interest in the team's history is thanks to a very special coach. Beginning my sophomore year, as a running back, I was fortunate enough to be mentored by coach Rick Staley. I still remember him telling us stories of years past, great players and games. He helped instill in all of us a respect for those in whose footsteps we were treading. Coach Staley was part of the Tornado program for twenty-six years, shaping the minds and abilities of countless young men. Sadly, we lost him in 2010. Without his influence on a fifteen-year-old kid back in 1992, I might not have been writing this now.

Finally, I need to thank my family for their endless support of my "projects," including my parents, especially my father, who gave in and let me play football in fourth grade. Most importantly, thank you to my wife and two boys, whose support and encouragement make all things possible.

INTRODUCTION

For well over one hundred years, the Dover-Phila football rivalry has excited fans on both sides of the Tuscarawas River. Ranking as Ohio's third-oldest rivalry, behind only Massillon-McKinley and Sandusky-Fremont Ross, the game exemplifies the strong emphasis on high school football that is typical of northeast Ohio. Beginning in 1896, when the rivals first squared off, the game has featured many special performances, great plays and fabulous finishes. The pages that follow are an attempt to chronicle some of these great moments. Whether you remember Paul Miskimen's field goal in 1946 to beat the Tornadoes, Don Watson's ninety-four-yard fumble return or Richard Sandilands's outstanding performances in 2004 and 2005, *The Dover-Phila Football Rivalry* holds something for football fans from all eras.

One of the most surprising facts about the long history of the Dover-Phila rivalry is how evenly matched the two teams have been throughout the decades. This point was truly hammered home in 2004 as the two teams lined up for the 100th matchup. Remarkably, the 100th meeting saw the teams tied at 45-45-9. What's even more interesting, though, is how they got to that point.

The more than one hundred years of rivalry can actually be broken down into two distinct eras, each dominated by a different team. In the first era, the Quakers were dominant, while in recent years the tide has turned toward the Tornadoes. From 1896 to 1958, the Quakers won thirty-two of the fifty-four games they played against their crosstown rival, the Tornadoes, while Dover won only fifteen. The two teams also tied seven times. Also

Introduction

during this era, we find the Quaker coaches with four of the five highest-winning percentages. Taking into account a minimum of three seasons at the helm, New Phila was led by Paul Hoerneman (80 percent), John Brickels (75 percent), George Pierce (67 percent) and Woody Hayes (63 percent), all prior to 1959. The only New Philadelphia coach from the modern era to crack the top five in win percentage is current coach Matt Dennison. In addition, the man whom many regard as New Phila's greatest coach, William "Bill" Kidd, coached all but two of his seasons prior to 1959, with a record of 82-48-8. Of Kidd's five losing seasons, three came in 1958, 1959 and 1960. Finally, quite possibly the greatest moment for New Philadelphia's program came in 1956, when the Quakers annihilated an injury-plagued Tornado team 72–0.

In every way that the Quakers dominated the first era of the rivalry, Dover has dominated the second. Beginning with their win in 1959, 36–0, the Dover Tornadoes have won thirty-six of fifty-three contests with New Philadelphia, and the two teams have tied twice. Much like the Quakers, many of the greatest Tornado coaches have come during this era. These include Bob Maltarich (with a win percentage of 77 percent), Dick Haines (74 percent), Tom Redman (68 percent) and current Head Coach Dan Ifft (78 percent). In 2006, Coach Ifft passed Dick Haines to become Dover's all-time leader in wins as a head coach. With Dover's recent dominance over its rival, it is easy to forget that New Phila once held the same advantage. One can only guess what the next era will hold for both teams.

Despite the two contrasting eras, you'll find a pretty even split between Dover and New Philadelphia wins in the chapters that follow. Coming into this project, there was no real emphasis on making sure that each team had a similar amount of wins represented. In the end, that is just how the book shaped up.

One aspect that has been a point of emphasis is trying to equally represent the two communities and their rich football traditions. Whenever an author or historian writes a book, there are bound to be those who question bias. As a Dover alumni and former football player for the Tornadoes, I know that many Phila fans will be skeptical as they begin reading. Nothing I can tell you at the beginning of this introduction is going to change that. All I can do is ask that you give the book a fair reading. In writing it, I've done my best to let the sources speak to me, to choose games that represent the best contests and to chronicle some of the game's best performances.

Introduction

Anytime you take on a topic as heated and as up for debate as this, there are bound to be those who disagree. In essence, that is the best part of a book like this. I can only hope that this will be a conversation starter for many discussions over the coming years. In the end, that's the best part of the rivalry—the fact that we care about it so deeply. It is what makes our communities special and gives our young men dreams of glory on crisp fall nights.

1
THE EARLY YEARS
1896–1929

1905: GROVER "DODE" ROSENBERRY AND C. PAUL TOWNSEND BECOME THE RIVALS' FIRST COACHES

The dawn of the 1904 season marked a first for both the Dover and New Philadelphia football teams. For the first time in their existence, both teams had head coaches to help guide them through practices and games. In both cases, each man was a volunteer, and both were also nearly young enough to play on the team.

New Philadelphia's first coach was C. Paul Townsend. He was a local man, possibly a millworker, and would've been nineteen or twenty when he took over as coach. Townsend remained at New Philadelphia for five seasons, compiling a record of 23-7-9. More importantly, he mentored future New Philadelphia head coaches Albert Senhauser (1909–12), Adam Schwab (1922) and Irwin Empfield (1919, 1922). Senhauser would compile a record of 24-12 while coach of New Phila, before heading to Dover, where his record was 7-9-3 in two seasons (1919–20). Senhauser is the only man to coach at both schools.

Not to be outdone by its rivals across the river, Dover also named its first head coach in 1904. Grover "Dode" Rosenberry was a former Dover student and football player. He was a member of the 1901 and 1902 football teams that went 1-0-1 and 4-2-1, respectively. Against New Philadelphia, his high school teams were 1-0-1, and he was part of the 1901 team that was the first ever to defeat the mighty Phils. Following his 1902 campaign with the Crimsons, Rosenberry quit

THE DOVER-PHILA FOOTBALL RIVALRY

The 1905 New Phila High School football team with Coach C. Paul Townsend pictured in the back row wearing a striped shirt. *Courtesy of the Quaker Foundation.*

The 1905 Dover High School football team with Coach Grover "Dode" Rosenberry pictured in the back row wearing a hat. *Courtesy of the Dover Historical Society.*

school to go to work in the Reeves Mill. Two years later, in 1904, he volunteered his time and services as Dover's first coach. At the time, he was only seventeen.

The lone matchup between the two first coaches ended, fittingly, in a tie. Coming into the game, New Philadelphia's team was highly favored, having tied Massillon and Coshocton and beaten Newark and a local mill team. The win against Newark two weeks prior to the game was an absolute beating, with New Philadelphia romping to a 31–0 victory.

Dover was 2-0 coming into the contest but had wins over less impressive opponents like the Dover Eagles and Newcomerstown. The game itself was rather uneventful, as New Philadelphia was able to move the ball, yet it always seemed to fall apart when it got within striking distance of the goal line. Dover never seems to have really threatened the superior New Phila team but managed a tie through ball control, field position and good punting.

After the game, New Philadelphia would go on to a successful season, finishing with four impressive victories over Cambridge, Alliance, Cambridge (again) and Wooster. Dover also finished well, going 2-0-1. Its final game of the season, and of Rosenberry's short coaching career at Dover, was a 49–0 clubbing of Girard.

Although his high school coaching career ended after only two years, Rosenberry continued to remain active on the local sports scene. He was an amateur boxer and played football for the local semipro Dover Giants. Later, he coached the Giants and worked locally as an official. When he finally moved on from sports, "Dode" Rosenberry developed a reputation locally as a restaurateur. His first restaurant was at 235 West Second Street in Dover. His second was a partnership with his brother, Samuel Rosenberry, and was at 234 Factory Street (Tuscarawas Avenue) in Dover. In 1929, Rosenberry lost his business in the Great Depression and was forced to return to the mill. Later, he moved to Indiana, where he lived out the rest of his days.

1908: Dover, 5; New Phila, 0:
The Beginning of a Rivalry

Although the Dover-Phila football rivalry began in 1896, it's pretty easy to argue that the rivalry didn't really materialize until 1908. That year marked the first real upset in the series and also the first real evidence that both towns had developed more than a passing interest in the game.

The Dover-Phila Football Rivalry

The 1908 New Philadelphia High School football team. *Courtesy of Denny Rubright.*

The 1908 Dover High School football team. *Courtesy of Denny Rubright.*

The Early Years

The 1908 New Philadelphia High School football team. *Courtesy of Denny Rubright.*

Coming into the contest, New Philadelphia was a powerhouse. It boasted a tough defense and a very respectable record of 4-1-1. Its only loss prior to the Dover-Phila game came at the hands of Oberlin Academy, by the score of 8–0. Furthermore, it had blown out opponents like Coshocton (53–0) and Steubenville (32–0). New Phila's defense was so good that it had been mentioned in Cleveland's *Plain Dealer* for its incredible record of twenty-six shutouts in its previous thirty-one games. During his five years as New Philadelphia's head football coach, C. Paul Townsend had compiled an overall record of 23-7-9.

During the same period, from 1904 to 1908, Dover fought to a record of 11-3-2. Unfortunately for Dover, eight of its eleven wins were in 1904 and 1905. Coming into the 1908 season, it had failed to field a team in 1907 and played only one game (a 0–0 tie against New Phila's reserves) in 1906. Dover's 1908 season, prior to the Dover-Phila game, had been one of ups and downs. It played a tough schedule with back-to-back road games against Massillon and Canton McKinley, holding its own (5–5) against Massillon but being blown out (53–0) by Canton. Things began to look up for Dover, though, on October 19, 1908. That was the day that Sherburne Wightman agreed to become Dover's second head coach.

Sherburne H. Wightman was the coach of the local semipro Dover Giants when he agreed to lead Dover's high school team through the final two games—a rematch against Massillon and the season finale against New Philadelphia and its daunting defense. Wightman was an Ohio boy but not from Tuscarawas County. He grew up in Cleveland, playing football for South High School. After graduation, Wightman attended the University of Chicago, where he was fortunate to play under legendary coach Amos Alonzo Stagg. Today, the NCAA Division III football championship is named the Stagg Bowl in Coach Stagg's honor.

Wightman would play two years under Stagg before transferring to Swarthmore College, from which he graduated in 1906. After college, Wightman returned to Ohio and became the head coach of the semipro Massillon Tigers football team. Under his guidance, Massillon racked up a record of 17-1-1 and won two Ohio State titles. When Massillon failed to organize a team in 1908, Wightman's services were available, and he landed in Dover as the coach of the Giants.

After taking over coaching duties at the high school, Wightman's impact was immediate. In his first game as coach, Coach Wightman's squad defeated Massillon (26–0). With only two weeks remaining until Dover faced the heavily favored New Philadelphia squad, Dover's big win over Massillon gave the locals hope that the boys from Canal Dover would give the county-seaters a game.

On Saturday, November 14, 1908, the game commenced between Dover and the heavily favored New Philadelphia squad. The game took place at the Tuscarawas County Fairgrounds with a large, enthusiastic crowd in attendance. Despite a chill in the air and lightly falling snow, nearly eighteen hundred fans are believed to have attended the game. In fact, there were so many people in attendance that a wire fence was built around the playing field to prevent any fan interference.

The game began with Dover kicking off to the New Philadelphia team, but disaster struck early for Phila's squad. New Philadelphia return man Reid Wilkin fumbled the opening kickoff. Dover cover man Ernest Godfrey recovered the ball deep in New Phila territory, and the Crimsons were in business. Only three plays later, Dover running back Hubert Casebeer struck pay dirt, scoring a touchdown for the Crimson and Gray. New Phila's vaunted defense had given up a touchdown on only the fourth play of the

The Early Years

game. Although the extra point kick failed, five points was all Dover would need. The Red and Black made one serious threat in the second half, driving to within sight of a touchdown, but a fumble on third down allowed Dover to regain possession near the goal line. Dover took over, running out the clock, and hung on to defeat the Red and Black.

While the game was memorable, it was the aftermath of Dover's upset victory that truly cemented the rivalry. The local *Tuscarawas Advocate* reported extensively on the celebratory events after the big game. At about eight o'clock on Saturday evening after the game, a streetcar full of Dover supporters got the bright idea to head on over to New Philadelphia and "rub it in" a little. The group, described as Dover boys, chartered a car, loaded up a band and prepared to parade around the New Philadelphia Square in celebration of their victory. Later, those involved in the provocation that followed would claim that their trip was only in response to New Phila's plans to do the same had they won the game. Others suggested that it was more than merrymaking that the Dover youths were looking to do. Some suggestions were put out that the Dover boys were looking for a fight with the New Phila fans, with whom they had words during halftime of the game.

Regardless of their intentions, the boys boarded a streetcar and headed to New Philadelphia. Upon arriving, the young men weren't able to make their way off the car. They were greeted by a throng of several hundred New Philadelphia fans anxious to stop the celebration before it ever began. Despite the presence of police, the streetcar was pelted with eggs, breaking several windows. To avoid further damage, the streetcar turned around, and the revelers returned to Dover. Luckily, no one was hurt.

In addition to the incident involving the streetcar, the budding rivalry was further fueled by speculation on the part of New Philadelphia that the Dover team had "bought" the officials. The week following the game, New Philadelphia superintendant G.C. Maurer protested the outcome of the game to the Ohio High School Athletic Association. He alleged that the field judge had usurped more authority than granted by the rules, that several officials had money wagered on the game and that someone from New Phila had sold the football team's signals to Dover. In response to Maurer's accusations, one of the officials did admit that one mistake was made in the contest. To Maurer's chagrin, the official, Carl Compton, conceded that on one penalty, New Philadelphia should have been penalized five yards instead of the fifteen that the officials had mistakenly marched off. In Compton's estimation, though, the penalty did not affect the game's outcome, and Dover won "fairly and squarely."

Between the streetcar of Dover gloaters and the contested outcome of the game, both schools soured on the rivalry following the 1908 season. The disputed game raised such a ruckus that the two teams would not play again until 1914, six years after the emotional 1908 Crimson and Gray victory.

Dover's Jacob and Ernest Godfrey

Lost in all the controversy of the 1908 Dover victory was the kindness shown by several New Philadelphia players to Dover's Jacob Godfrey. Jacob "Jake" Godfrey was injured during the 1908 Dover-Phila game and seems to have spent some time recovering from his injury. In the week following the game, Godfrey was visited by several New Philadelphia players. The young men displayed great character in rising above the controversy to visit their opponent and even bring him a bouquet of flowers.

Ernest Godfrey. *Courtesy of Denny Rubright.*

The Early Years

Godfrey's brother, Ernest, was only a sophomore on that 1908 team and would never again meet the Red and Black on the field. Following the 1908 game, the teams wouldn't play again until 1914. Ernest, though, would go on to have an outstanding career as a player and later a coach. After graduating from Dover in 1911, Godfrey went on to the Ohio State University, where he played both football and basketball for the Buckeyes.

After college, Ernest Godfrey accepted the head-coaching job at Wooster High School. This would be short-lived, as Godfrey only remained one year at Wooster before moving on to Wittenberg College in 1916. At Wittenberg, Godfrey became the college's first full-time football and basketball coach. During his tenure, the Wittenberg Tigers tasted great success and even a few undefeated seasons.

In 1929, after building quite a reputation as a coach, Godfrey accepted a position as an assistant at Ohio State. He remained a Buckeye assistant for the next thirty-three years, retiring in 1962. During his time at Ohio State, Godfrey coached a number of Buckeye greats, including Lou "the Toe" Groza and Heisman Trophy–winner Vic Janowicz. Godfrey also had the distinction of watching fellow Dover native and Buckeye quarterback Frank Ellwood win a National Championship with the team in 1954.

Following his retirement from coaching in 1962, Godfrey couldn't stay away from the football field. In 1968, he was hired by former Buckeye and current Cincinnati Bengal head coach Paul Brown to work with the kickers and punters during the pre-season. Godfrey died in 1980 at the age of eighty-six. He is a member of the Wittenberg, Ohio State, Ohio High School Coaches Association and College Football Halls of Fame.

1916: Dover, 7; New Phila, 0

After a six-year layoff from 1908 to 1914, the rivalry again gained steam in 1916. The layoff was due to bad blood generated after the 1908 game. Two separate incidents produced a reluctance to play on the part of both sides. After their big win in 1908, several Dover boys rode to the square in New Philadelphia to taunt the defeated city and nearly started a riot. In addition, New Philadelphia superintendant G.C. Maurer protested the outcome of the game, angering fans from Dover.

The Dover-Phila Football Rivalry

The 1916 Dover High School football team. *Courtesy of Denny Rubright.*

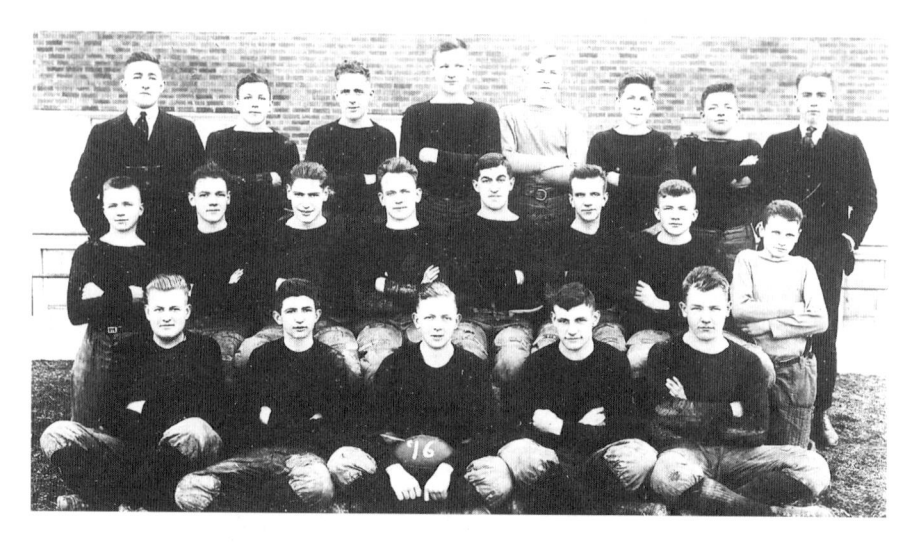

The 1916 New Philadelphia High School football team. *Courtesy of the Quaker Foundation.*

The Early Years

The 1916 New Philadelphia High School Manager Schoemaker, Captain Cable and Coach Wilson. *Courtesy of the Quaker Foundation.*

Resuming the rivalry in 1914, Dover had very little success against New Phila and Coach George Pierce. In the stretch from 1913 through 1915, Pierce compiled a record of 21-6-4, including a 10-1 record in 1915. That year, the only loss New Philadelphia suffered was a 13–0 defeat at the hands of the Massillon Tigers. The year 1915 also included two drubbings of Dover, 39–0 on October 23 and 42–0 on Thanksgiving Day (November 25).

Dover was quite a different story in contrast to its powerful crosstown rivals. Since the 1908 season, Dover had compiled an overall record of 9-19-4. In three of those years, 1910–12, it didn't even field a team. Despite these lean years, things began to look up for the Crimsons as the 1916 season approached.

On June 8, 1916, Dover hired Fred Hart to serve as its new football coach. Hart was paid a respectable sum of $1,000 for his services. He also became the first football coach to serve as a member of the faculty. On Labor Day 1916, the community rejoiced as Dover opened its brand-new Roosevelt High School on Fifth Street. The new high school sat alongside the now dated Oak Grove School and featured fifty rooms. The total cost for the new school was nearly $200,000, and once completed, it was considered one of the finest schools in the state.

The Dover-Phila Football Rivalry

Things were looking up for Dover's football team as well. The players had reason to hope for a better showing against their archrival in 1916 as they returned seven starters from the previous year. These included halfback Edward Heikes, captain and right guard Nelson McMillan and kicking specialist and leading scorer Fred "Fritz" Weber.

Coming into the first matchup with Phila, Dover was off to a fast start. It held a record of 4-1 under its new coach with a prolific offense that scored ninety-six points in its first five games. The week before the game against New Phila, it blew out Coshocton 41–0. New Philadelphia, on the other hand, had struggled mightily. It was 1-3 on the season and had suffered a 28–0 defeat at the hands of the Massillon Tigers in the week before the big game.

The week leading up to the game was one of the most eventful in the history of the rivalry. Both teams brought in additional help to ready the boys for battle. For Dover, that expertise was provided by Red Fleming, a star on the Massillon Tigers professional football team. To further gain an edge, beginning on Wednesday, Dover moved its practice into the country outside town to prevent New Philadelphia "spies" from watching its preparations. According to a few of the players who chased them off, several New Phila fans were seen observing Dover's practice through binoculars earlier in the week.

New Philadelphia also made special preparations the week of the big game. It, too, worried about spies, but instead of moving practice, it set about recruiting and organizing groups of students to patrol the perimeter of its practice field and chase off any Dover fans.

Not to be outdone by Dover's guest coach, New Philadelphia brought in twenty-eight-year-old Jim Thorpe of the professional Canton Bulldogs as a guest coach for the week of the Dover-Phila game. At the time he arrived in New Philadelphia, Thorpe was already a big-name star. He played both professional football and baseball and won gold medals in both the pentathlon and decathlon at the 1912 Stockholm Olympics. Thorpe's presence would bring three championships to the Canton Bulldogs, including one in 1916 over Red Fleming's Tigers. In addition to his athletic achievements, Thorpe was also well known for the hefty sum he commanded in return for his talents. During the 1915 season, Canton agreed to pay Jim Thorpe the astronomical sum of $250 per game.

The Early Years

When game day finally arrived, the players were greeted by Dover alumni Daniel McBride. Right before kickoff, McBride, a Dover graduate the previous spring, lofted two "doves of peace" into the air. The doves, draped in the Dover's school colors of crimson and gray, flew directly toward Dover's end zone and over one of the goalposts. Ironically, it would be a lone score in this end zone only a short while later that would decide the outcome of the game.

Much like the 1908 game, the last time the Crimson and Gray was victorious over New Phila, the big play came early. As time wound down in the first half, Dover halfback Ed Heikes turned the corner, eluding five New Philadelphia players, and scored on an eighty-yard run. Controversy soon erupted, though, when both time keepers claimed that time had expired before Dover set the play in motion. The referee, on the other hand, claimed that Dover got off the snap before time expired, and therefore the play—and thus the touchdown—would count. Although New Philadelphia walked off the field while the officials conferred, it would later return as the referee won out, and Fritz Weber kicked the extra point to give Dover a 7–0 lead. Heikes would go on to rush for well over one hundred yards that afternoon, becoming the first Dover back to cross the century mark in the big game.

Although no one would score in the second half, Dover threatened several times, including a drive that went all the way to the Phila five-yard line before a fumble returned possession to the Red and Black. Dover also missed three field goals in the game. New Philadelphia, on the other hand, saw little or no success on the offensive side of the ball. It managed only three first downs and never threatened to tie the game.

The aftermath of the October 1916 game brought about another unwelcome celebration in New Philadelphia. Once again, enthusiastic—and somewhat misguided—Dover boys made their way across the river into New Philadelphia. As they traversed the streets of New Philadelphia, the young men showered the city's residents with battle cries and noise from their horns. Their enthusiasm was answered with eggs, cabbages and lemons. Things turned especially ugly after several verbal and physical confrontations. The Dover boy's bravado led to the projectiles changing from vegetables and fruits to bricks. By the time they returned to Dover, many of their automobiles were badly damaged, with broken windshields, headlights and dented doors. As the local *Daily Times* pointed out, if Dover won the big game a little more often, perhaps it wouldn't feel the need to gloat as much.

Later in the year, New Philadelphia had a chance at revenge against the Crimson and Gray, but both teams came up empty. The rematch, played on Thanksgiving Day, November 30, 1916, was a 0–0 tie.

1919: New Phila, 10; Dover, 7; and New Phila, 1; Dover, 0—A Very Controversial Year

The beginning of the school year in 1919, and thus of football season, must have come as a welcome return to normalcy after the uncertainty that was 1918. The year 1918 saw the end of World War I and one of the worst outbreaks of pandemic disease on record. Lasting from June 1917 until December 1920, the 1918 flu pandemic was a strain of the Spanish flu. Unlike previous outbreaks, this particular strain was especially deadly to young, relatively healthy individuals. In all, 50 million people died from the flu, and a whopping 500 million were infected. These numbers represent the staggering figures of a 3 percent death rate and a 28 percent infection rate worldwide.

Closer to home, the flu hit both school districts, with all classes being cancelled beginning October 14, 1918, and not resuming until December

The 1919 New Philadelphia High School football team. *Courtesy of Denny Rubright.*

The Early Years

New Philadelphia coach Irwin "Dale" Empfield. *Courtesy of Denny Rubright.*

30. On the field, the epidemic virtually cancelled the 1918 season. Dover managed to play three games, going 1-2, with New Philadelphia finishing 2-0, with a 1–0 forfeit over Massillon ending its season.

With these tragic events as the backdrop, you can only imagine that both schools were eagerly anticipating a return to normalcy in 1919. While they did return to the field in the fall of 1919, normal is not an effective adjective for describing the bizarre events for both schools.

Coming into the 1919 season, Dover had little luck against the stronger New Phila program. Since its win in 1916, Dover had struggled to a 0-2-1 record against the county-seaters. Included in this total were two losses to New Phila by a combined score of 108–0. In fact, Dover had not scored against its rivals since the 1916 win.

New Philadelphia, on the other hand, had been strong, posting a record of 10-0-1 since its loss to Dover. Prior to the opening of the season, New

Philadelphia had hired hometown boy and 1908 graduate Irwin "Dale" Empfield to be its coach. At the time of his hiring, Empfield was a recently returned veteran of World War I.

Dover, in turn, also dipped into the ranks of World War I veterans and hired its own alumni in the person of Norman Zeller. Zeller was young at the time of his hiring, having graduated from Dover only three years earlier in 1916. Although neither coach would enjoy a long tenure at his alma mater, Zeller's coaching career was exceptionally short. He spent only one game as Dover's coach. After a very poor showing against the Uhrichsville Tigers (a 6–0 loss), the Dover Board of Education voted to disband the team, effectively ending Dover's season on September 25.

After several weeks had gone by, with the players still clamoring to play, the school board reconsidered. Superintendant Sam Mase later said, "We left the matter of a Dover High School football team entirely up to the players. I believe the boys should be allowed to play if they want." On Monday, October 13, Dover's gridders returned to the field with one notable exception. Norman Zeller was out as head coach. His replacement was 1906 New Philadelphia High School graduate and former Red and Black coach Albert "Dutch" Senhauser.

Only five days after practice resumed, Dover faced off against the Red and Black. Surprisingly, the game was close even in light of Dover's long layoff. Although New Philadelphia was able to successfully move the ball at will in the first half, Dover's bend-don't-break defense held it to only three points. Three times New Philadelphia drove to deep within Dover territory, and two of the three times it came up entirely empty. Dover, on the other hand, may not have moved the ball as effectively as the Phils, but it was able to squeak out a 7–3 halftime lead on a touchdown run by senior left halfback Eugene Rippel.

During the third period, neither team seemed capable of moving the ball. At the end of three, the score remained 7–3 in Dover's favor. The turning point came late in the game with New Philadelphia seemingly bogged down at the thirty-five-yard line. Even with New Philadelphia in no danger of scoring, Dover made a player substitution that was deemed illegal. The penalty for this illegal substitution turned the game. Instead of getting the ball back to run out the clock, Dover was penalized half the distance to the goal line, or thirty-five yards, to give New Philadelphia the ball on Dover's thirty-five-yard line. With the momentum shift, New Phila came alive, and quarterback Joseph Hurst scampered in for the game-winning score.

Although the thirty-five-yard penalty seems rather harsh, it is worth noting that Dover did not protest the outcome. It appears that in those days, once a player was removed from a game, he was not permitted to return. Dover did just that and suffered the consequences.

After this memorable showdown, both teams went on to play their regular slate of games before they reunited for their season-ending Thanksgiving Day battle. During this stretch, New Philadelphia did something extraordinary. On November 8, it set a state record for the worst blowout in Ohio high school football history.

Prior to the record-setting contest, no one would have expected this outcome, as Caldwell was rumored to have been undefeated in the previous four years. From the opening kickoff, New Philadelphia started scoring. It led 57–0 at halftime and 108–0 at the end of the third period. Even with the second-stringers in, the Caldwell team could do nothing to stop the New Philadelphia juggernaut that racked up a state record 154 points to Caldwell's 0. Leading the way in the romp for New Phila was Russell Beichley, who scored seven times, including four interceptions returned for touchdowns. Altogether, New Philadelphia racked up a total of twenty-four touchdowns.

Although the fans didn't see a record-setting night, the outcome of the rivals' Thanksgiving 1919 meeting was no less bizarre. The game itself lasted only seven minutes. After a disputed call by the referee, Dover's coach, Albert Senhauser, pulled his team off the field, walked up Wabash Hill and headed back to Dover.

At the time of the disputed play, New Philadelphia held a 7–0 lead on a thirty-yard fumble return by Russell Beichley. After being stopped in Dover territory, New Philadelphia was forced to punt. On the disputed play, the kicker launched the ball into the end zone. The umpire picked up the ball to put it into play, but before he could do so, New Phila's Beichley grabbed the ball out of his hands and touched it down. As everyone stared in shock, the referee signaled a Red and Black touchdown. Although no one had touched the ball prior to the umpire, the touchdown was upheld. In protest, coach Senhauser marched his team off the field and back to Dover, forfeiting the game.

While today we would recognize this play as a touchback, the interpretation of the rule was not as clear in 1919. New Philadelphia claimed that the disputed play was not a punt but a free kick, allowing it to recover and score. It seems the referee agreed, as the play—and thus the outcome of the game—stood.

Later, football experts Harry Edwards of the *Cleveland Plain Dealer* and legendary authority Walter Camp weighed in on Dover's side. Despite what the experts said, Senhauser was guilty of removing his team from the field and effectively forfeiting the sixteenth game in the rivalry. Number seventeen wouldn't come until 1921, as the disputed call again caused the two schools to sever relations.

Albert "Dutch" Senhauser: The Only Man to Coach Both Dover and New Phila

Albert "Dutch" Senhauser is an anomaly in the history of the Dover-Phila rivalry. He was a coach, a businessman, a war veteran and even a boxing promoter. He is also the only man to serve as head coach of both Dover and New Philadelphia.

Albert "Dutch" Senhauser. *Courtesy of Denny Rubright.*

The Early Years

The Senhauser story began when Albert's grandfather Gustavus moved to the area in 1854. After arriving in New Philadelphia, he worked with John Chapin in the dry goods business before partnering with Nicholas Kaderly to found the firm of Senhauser and Kaderly. In 1882, Senhauser was confident enough to strike out on his own in the clothing business. His first store was in New Philadelphia, and later subsequent generations of the family went on to open branches in Dover, Cambridge, Steubenville and Mansfield.

Albert "Dutch" Senhauser was born in New Philadelphia just a few years after his grandfather opened his clothing store, and he attended the city's public schools. As a senior at New Phila, he was a member of the 1905 Red and Black football team that put together a stellar campaign, going 6-0-3 and tying Dover (0–0). After graduation, Senhauser attended Oberlin College and later studied voice while living in New York City. Long after his days in athletics were over, Senhauser was well known locally for his beautiful singing voice.

After returning to the area in 1909, Senhauser replaced his mentor, C. Paul Townsend, becoming New Philadelphia's second head football coach. In his four seasons as coach, the Phils put together a very respectable record of 24-12. Unfortunately, Senhauser's four seasons at the helm of the New Philadelphia program were at a time when Dover and New Philadelphia had severed all ties athletically. It was only in 1914, two seasons after Senhauser left the team, that the two schools would renew their rivalry.

In 1918, as World War I raged on in Europe, Senhauser enlisted and joined the war effort. He returned eight months later and resumed work in the family business. It was an exciting time for the Senhauser Clothing chain, as the following year the family opened a store in downtown Dover at 236 Factory Street (Tuscarawas Avenue). It was probably while running the family's Dover store that Senhauser heard about the opportunity to get back into coaching.

Coming into the 1919 season, Dover had brought in alumnus and Mount Union graduate Norman Zeller to coach its team. Zeller's coaching career was short-lived, though, as the school board decided to cancel the Crimsons' season after only one game, an embarrassing loss to Uhrichsville, 6–0. Several weeks later, the school board reconsidered, allowing the players to resume practice, but with one change: Zeller was replaced by Senhauser as the team's head coach.

The thirty-three-year-old Senhauser would remain at Dover for two years, compiling a record of 7-9-3 overall and 0-2 against his alma mater. Later, he would coach a semipro team of former Dover and New Philadelphia players and work as a promoter for the boxer the Alabama Kid.

1922: Dover, 7; New Phila, 6

Although New Phila fell just short against Dover in the rivalry game, 1922 was a very eventful year for the Red and Black. That year, the football team had four head coaches. Beginning the season, it was led by promising head coach Allen Snyder. Snyder had led the Phils in the previous year, compiling an impressive record of 6-2-1, including a 13–0 shutout of Dover. Controversy soon erupted, though, when several school board members objected to Snyder's coaching stipend. In addition to his pay as a teacher at New Philadelphia, Snyder was also set to receive $500 for his services

The 1922 Dover High School football team. *Courtesy of Denny Rubright.*

The Early Years

as football coach. Many of the same people also objected to the idea that Snyder was in charge of all athletics at the school. They argued that this was too much power for one person.

In response to the complaints, Snyder resigned his position before the season began. Even though a petition was circulated by his supporters in the community, the damage was done; Snyder and his wife left the area. The young couple moved to Bowling Green University, where he coached for a year before returning to his home state of Pennsylvania.

To replace Snyder, the school district hired Columbus native Charles Farry. Farry had spent the previous two years as coach at Zanesville. The new coach was quickly impressed with his squad as the team got off to a great start against Wadsworth High School, trouncing it 33–0. Unfortunately for Farry, the momentum didn't carry over from that first big victory, and New Philadelphia dropped two of its next three contests. Encouraged by tough losses to Kent (13–19) and Alliance (6–7), naysayers again surfaced calling for Farry's job. The young coach must have had a thin skin, as only four games into his coaching career at New Phila he resigned. Although he would go on to teach math for many years in the district, Farry never again returned to the coaching ranks.

For the third time in the fall of 1922, New Philadelphia found itself looking for a head coach. This time, it decided to hire not one man but two. Halfway through the season, it hired co-head coaches Irwin Empfield and Adam Schwab. Empfield was a recognizable name with coaching experience (he was the Red and Black head coach in 1919), and Schwab was a well-known local businessman. More important than their current occupations, both men had played together at New Phila under coach C. Paul Townsend. Both men were also teammates at Washington and Jefferson College in Pennsylvania. Together, they led New Philadelphia to a 3-2 record the remainder of the season.

Dover, on the other hand, had a little more stability than its rival across the river. It was led by second-year coach, William Trautwein. In 1921, Trautwein led the Crimson and Gray to a 3-4 record. The year 1922 looked to be a promising one, though, as Dover returned eight lettermen, including captain Millard Groh, running back Anthony "Tony" Nigro and punter Eugene "Scrap Iron" Young. All of Dover's home games that year were played at the fairgrounds, while practices rotated between the fairgrounds, Oak Grove School and the Reeves Diamond in front of the Reeves Manufacturing Company.

The Dover-Phila Football Rivalry

Coming into the big game, Dover had struggled, losing three of its last four contests, while New Philadelphia had come together with wins over Mount Vernon and Cambridge. New Philadelphia's overall record was 5-3, even with all the coaching instability, while Dover stood at 4-4. On Thanksgiving eve, the day before the big game, Dover held what was possibly its first real pep rally in the high school auditorium. Attendees were treated to speeches by community leaders like Jacob Godfrey, Dr. Max Shaweker and Joe Streb. The faithful also enjoyed a lunch and a dance following the pep rally.

Whether it was the ideal weather or the similar records, a record crowd of thirty-five hundred turned out for the game at Tuscora Park. New Philadelphia's fans were not disappointed as the Red and Black took an early lead. A trick play got New Philadelphia to the five before Dover's defense tightened up. Although it took a one-yard touchdown on fourth down, New Philadelphia's 128-pound sophomore running back Clyde Mathias plunged in for the game's first score. A missed kick on the next play gave the county-seaters a 6–0 lead at the end of the first quarter.

The second quarter of the rivalry game saw the only other score that afternoon. With a little over two minutes to play before halftime, Dover

The 1922 Dover-Phila Game. *Courtesy of Denny Rubright.*

The Early Years

New Philadelphia goes in for the first score of the 1922 rivalry game. *Courtesy of Denny Rubright.*

Dover's Tony Nigro scores to tie the game 6–6. Dover would take the lead after a successful dropkick by Glen Willoughby. *Courtesy of Denny Rubright.*

The Dover-Phila Football Rivalry

running back Tony Nigro broke loose for a fifteen-yard touchdown. On the very next play, Dover's kicker Glen Willoughby dropkicked the ball through the upright, giving the Crimsons a 7–6 halftime lead. This would be all the scoring the spectators would see that afternoon. Despite an impressive aerial attack by New Phila in the fourth quarter, neither team managed to score again. The 7–6 win gave Dover its first victory ever on New Philadelphia's home field.

In the aftermath of the game, Dover's community celebrated heartily. Banquets were held at many local restaurants for the boys. During one week alone, they attended four celebrations in their honor. The weeks after the game also proved especially profitable for two of Dover's young gridders. Both Eugene "Scrap Iron" Young and Tony Nigro were given handsome rewards for their efforts. Young's mother set up a bank account with $700 for the young man, while Nigro's father, Nick, gave him cash in the amount of $500. Not bad for 1922.

Following his career at Dover, Young chose to attend Notre Dame and play for legendary coach Knute Rockne. His football career at the university was short-lived, though, as he broke his leg during spring practice his freshman year. Despite this setback, he still managed to become an accomplished runner for the Irish, albeit not on the gridiron. Young competed as a member of the track and cross-country teams.

Even after his football-playing days were over, Young kept a good relationship with Coach Rockne and later worked as the school's first full-time athletic trainer. In this capacity, he was involved with the team during their 1930 and 1943 National Championship seasons. After leaving Notre Dame in 1945, Young continued to work as an athletic trainer first for the Pittsburgh Steelers and later with the Detroit Lions.

Dover's coach William Trautwein also went on to do great things after his time in the Tuscarawas Valley. Trautwein moved to Athens, Ohio, where he served as the head basketball coach from 1939 to 1949 and assisted on the football coaching staff for the Bobcats. In 1941, Trautwein's upstart Ohio University basketball team finished as runners-up in the National Invitation Tournament held in New York City's Madison Square Garden.

The Early Years

1928: Quaker Stadium Is Dedicated

The idea for a new stadium for the people of New Philadelphia was first hatched in 1926 by the high school's faculty manager, William Fishel. Several weeks later, Fishel bumped into Senator W.G. Nickles and shared his idea about building a modern facility for the Phila faithful. The ball started rolling, and Nickles, who was on the park board, invited Fishel to the next board meeting. After much discussion and several more meetings, a location was chosen and details were worked out.

Work began on the new stadium a year later, on July 25, 1927. The work was difficult because of the tendency of the low-lying field to flood. Much of the area had to be built up with gravel and topsoil. In addition to the stadium, a cinder track, wooden bleachers and two ticket booths were added to the site as well. The total cost of the stadium grew to $17,000. In all, the new stadium was capable of seating twenty-five hundred fans.

On Saturday, September 30, 1928, New Philadelphia played its first game in its newly dedicated Quaker Stadium. The game against Wooster was Phila's second of the year. In the previous week, it had been beaten handily by Toronto, 12–0.

On the field, New Phila was led by first-year head coach Henry Craine, who would remain at the school only two years, putting together an overall record of 7-9-3. Prior to coaching at New Phila, Craine was the head coach at Cleveland Heights High School. The Quaker squad that year returned only six lettermen. They were led by Fred "Fritz" Alexander, Donald Knauss, Jonas Rohrbach, Ernest Wheatley and captain Adolphus Hensel. Unfortunately, injuries haunted the Quakers in 1928, and they would post only two victories and score a paltry total of eighteen points all season.

Although the Red and Black would have a tough season, on that fall day they put everything together to defeat Wooster 6–0. After a scoreless first half, the game-breaking play came as Wooster lined up to punt in the third period. The Wooster line faltered, and New Phila's "Fritz" Alexander barreled through, heading straight for the Wooster punter. Although the punter did get off the kick, it slammed squarely into the shoulder of the diving Alexander. In a heads-up play, New Phila's Jonas Rohrbach scooped up the ball and ran in for the touchdown. Although an extra point pass to Rohrbach would fail, the Quaker quarterback holds the distinction of scoring the stadium's first touchdown.

The rest of the game was similar to the first half, and neither team managed another score, allowing New Philadelphia to win its first game in the new stadium 6–0. In an interesting note, not all of the fans who came out for that first game had tickets. In an article that ran the day after the first game, the newspaper criticized the twenty-five automobiles parked on Broadway hill that took in the first game for free. The paper was critical of the "cheapskates" who didn't want to pay for admission into the new stadium.

2
TWO DECADES OF OUTSTANDING PLAYERS

1930–1949

1930: Dover, 13; New Phila, 7

Like many of the years you'll find chronicled within these pages, 1930 was an important one not only because it resulted in an exciting close game between two rivals but also because of the interesting developments off the field.

Beginning early in the summer of 1930, it was rumored that New Philadelphia was planning to install lights at Quaker Stadium. The interest seems to have stemmed from a game the Quakers played the previous year against Salem High School. In 1929, Salem became the first Ohio high school to play night games under the lights. Prior to its matchup, Salem inquired if the Quakers would be willing to move the game to Salem and play under the lights. Although New Phila declined, not wanting to lose a home game, the seed was planted. By August 1930, New Philadelphia superintendent Franklin Geiger was willing to confirm that the Quakers were indeed in the process of installing lights. A short time later, ten sixty-foot poles were set and topped with four fifteen-hundred-watt bulbs each.

In addition to the lights, New Philadelphia also made several other additions to their two-year-old stadium, including adding bleachers in the east end for the band and a concession stand that sold hotdogs and popcorn. The upgrades were impressive, and spectators couldn't wait to come out and see the improvements. New Phila's first game under the lights came on

THE DOVER-PHILA FOOTBALL RIVALRY

The 1930 Dover High School football team. *Courtesy of the Dover Historical Society.*

September 19, 1930. The game, a 6–0 win over Dennison, was attended by over three thousand people.

Dover also made some improvements prior to the 1930 season but nothing as sensational as the Quaker Stadium updates. The Crimson and Gray came into the game sporting new uniforms. They featured gray jerseys with crimson stripes, khaki-colored pants, scarlet and gray socks and yellow and black helmets.

While the uniforms may have been new, one constant for the Crimsons was third-year head coach August "Gus" Peterka. Coming into the 1930 season, Peterka had a record of 8-8-4 in his tenure as coach. In addition to his eight wins, he had split his two matchups against the Red and Black. Assisting in the coaching duties was Fred "Fritz" Weber. Peterka's team was led by captain Trevor Rees and returning lettermen Don Foutz and Dale Godfrey. A relative unknown on Dover's team that year was a young freshman by the name of Frank "Doc" Kelker.

On the Quaker side, Coach Henry Craine did not return in 1930 after a 7-9-3 record in two seasons. Craine was replaced by new coach Ralph Bauer. Bauer, a native of Springfield, Ohio, played college ball under Dover's own Ernest Godfrey at Wittenberg before moving to the area to

Two Decades of Outstanding Players

coach at Newcomerstown in 1928. Although his record was only average in the southern Tuscarawas town, his time at Newcomerstown is notable for one reason. While there, he coached future New Philadelphia and legendary Ohio State coach Wayne "Woody" Hayes. In addition to Bauer, the Quakers also brought in Wittenberg College student John Brickels as an assistant. The new coaches were helped by eight returning lettermen, including quarterback Harold "Abie" Rolli and halfback Wendall Byrd.

Despite all of the exciting happenings off the field, neither team had a stellar record coming into the big game. Dover's record was an unimpressive 3-4 after a victory the previous week over Bauer's old Newcomerstown team, 19–0, while New Philadelphia stood at 5-4 with wins in three of its last four outings.

The week of the big game brought exceptionally cold temperatures and snow to the Tuscarawas Valley. On Tuesday night, a front moved through that dropped heavy ice and snow on Quaker Stadium. A small army of volunteers turned out the next day to prepare the field for the Thanksgiving Day tilt, but their efforts would go for naught. The Thanksgiving Day game was postponed on Thursday morning, when the mercury dropped to a bone-chilling four degrees.

Despite the extreme conditions, not everyone was convinced that cancelling the traditional Turkey Day afternoon game was the right decision. Many fans criticized those in charge. Local sportswriter Hal Jenkins accused Dover of ulterior motives. He claimed that the real reason behind the game's postponement was the worry over attendance due to the frigid temperatures. Surprisingly, Jenkins's accusation was answered in a public letter written by Dover superintendant Samuel Mase, who disputed Jenkins claim that the postponement was driven by worry over the receipts at the gate. As Mase put it, "The receipts on Thursday, despite the bad weather, would probably have been greater than they will be on Saturday, no matter what kind of weather develops." By Saturday morning, the weather had warmed up, and Superintendant Mase's assertion was proven correct. The smallest crowd in a decade showed up for the rivalry, with only 2,080 paid admissions.

With the opening kickoff, New Phila made up for lost time as it drove all the way down to Dover's one-yard line. Primed to score the game's first touchdown, the Red and Black made a costly error. A bad snap by center Melvin Carpenter bounced off the shoulder of Joe Zurcher and was recovered by Dover freshman "Doc" Kelker. Dover took over possession and dodged a bullet.

Dover would not be so lucky on New Philadelphia's next drive. After a Dover punt, New Phila's halfback, Wendall Byrd, hit Paul Olmstead with a fourteen-yard pass to set up a touchdown run by quarterback Harold Rolli. At the end of the first quarter, the score stood at 7–0 Quakers.

Although Dover failed to do much with the ball for most of the first half, it got things going at the end of the second quarter. On its scoring drive, Don Foutz rushed for forty-eight yards and the game-tying score as he plunged in from the three yard-line. With seventeen seconds left in the second quarter, the teams were tied at 7–7.

The third quarter proved uneventful for both squads, and at the end of three, the score remained deadlocked at 7–7. Dover's game winner in the fourth quarter came on a trick play by Foutz, Dover's punter and star running back. After lining up to punt, Foutz instead dropped back to pass, lofting the ball thirty-five yards downfield to James Smith. Smith broke several tackles, rumbling twelve more yards and carrying a Quaker defender across the goal line for the game-winning score. The forty-seven-yard pass was Dover's only completion that afternoon.

Although the Quakers mounted one last threat against their crosstown rivals, the Crimson and Gray held on to win after Kelker tackled Joe Zurcher on the game's final play. Individually, Dover was led by Foutz's 98 yards on eighteen carries, while New Phila's quarterback Harold Rolli completed eight of fifteen passes for 108 yards.

1931–1933: Dover's Era of Champions

Perhaps no era in the history of Dover High School was more magical than that from 1931 to 1933. During that three-year stretch, Dover won a state basketball championship, compiled a record of 30-1 on the football field and produced a band that won the 1933 National Championship.

While the accomplishments listed above are always a team effort, a truly exceptional team is only possible with outstanding talent. In that short three-year stretch, Dover produced three of its best talents ever on the football field. Although these three never played together, they still are remembered for their remarkable efforts that made Dover a championship city.

Two Decades of Outstanding Players

The one constant for all of the sports championships in the early 1930s was Dover coach Herman "Bup" Rearick. Rearick was a hometown boy, a 1927 graduate of Dover High who excelled at both football and basketball under Dover coach Joe Hermann. He was the quarterback on the 1926 team and a starter on the 1927 State Championship basketball team. With his father employed at the Reeves Mill, Rearick held strong working-class values. These values and a commitment to out-hustle and out-work his opponents translated to great success on the playing field.

After high school, Rearick attended Wittenberg College, where he played for fellow Dover alumni Ernie Godfrey. As a guard on Wittenberg's basketball team, he was named the team captain his senior year. Shortly before his graduation from Wittenberg, on May 28, 1931, Rearick was hired as Dover's head football and basketball coach. Between 1931 and 1937, "Bup" compiled an overall record of 51-13-4, with his best years coming from 1931 to 1934. During that stretch, Rearick's teams put together a streak of twenty-nine consecutive victories.

Rearick's tenure began with two of Dover's all-time greats on his squad. That year, his team was led by senior halfback and kicker Don Foutz and outstanding end Frank "Doc" Kelker. The team posted a record of 10-1, with seven consecutive wins after a week-three defeat by Wooster. Despite all the talent on that 1931 team, its undisputed star and team leader was Don Foutz.

Don Foutz is regarded by many local football experts as one of the greatest players ever to suit up for the Crimson and Gray. He was a talented kicker and an amazing "big game" halfback. During his senior season in 1931, he routinely averaged more than 42 yards per punt during games. Foutz also had a knack for saving his best rushing performances for big games. While he racked up 209 yards rushing against Uhrichsville, he saved his best for the final game of the season against the archrival New Philadelphia.

In the 1930 game against New Philadelphia, Foutz tallied 98 yards. In his final game for Dover against the Red and Black in 1931, Foutz put on a record-breaking performance, rushing 38 times for 232 yards and three touchdowns. This performance came on a wet and muddy field and led to a 27–6 Dover win.

In 1932, Dover's team was even better. Frank "Doc" Kelker was joined by his twin brother, Fred "Spider" Kelker, and twins Dale and Don Godfrey. Don Godfrey, who was the nephew of Rearick's coach at Wittenberg, was the starting quarterback that year on a team that went 10-0. Despite all of the talent, no one was more impressive than "Doc" Kelker. To this day, he is regarded by many as the best football player Dover ever produced.

Frank Kelker's story began in the small Florida community of Woodsville. Here, he and his twin brother, Fred, were born and lived the first two years of their lives. Even though the boys were twins, they were very different. Frank grew to be a hulking six-foot-two and 195 pounds, while his brother Fred only reached five-foot-ten, 160 pounds. When they were growing up, most people who didn't know the family assumed that Frank and his older brother John were twins, not the much smaller Fred.

To get away from the stunted opportunities and racial tensions of Florida in the 1920s, Frank's father moved the family to Tuscarawas County, where he began working at the Reeves Mill. After their move to Dover, both twins received the nicknames they would carry for the rest of their lives. Fred nicknamed his twin "Doc," while he received the name "Spike." "Spike" was later changed to "Spider," and both men were known in the community as Doc and Spider, not Frank and Fred.

Among "Doc" Kelker's many athletic achievements, he led the 1933 basketball team to a State Championship, led the football team to a 30-1

Dover's football team is seen practicing at the fairgrounds, circa 1931. Frank "Doc" Kelker is pictured in the foreground. *Courtesy of Dave Contini.*

Two Decades of Outstanding Players

record between 1931 and 1933, batted .521 for the baseball team that went 23-4 during the 1932-33 season and was once clocked at 9.9 seconds in the one-hundred-yard dash. After his career at Dover, "Doc" went on to play for Western Reserve University (Case Western Reserve University) in Cleveland. At Case, Kelker won nine varsity letters and was named to five all-American football teams. Perhaps his greatest accomplishments, though, came as a person. During Cleveland's Hough Riots in 1965, Kelker was serving as the executive director of the Cedar Addison Branch of the YMCA. Despite the rioting, the Addison Branch, which is located at the heart of the Hough Neighborhood, was not damaged or threatened. Kelker's accomplishments made him a role model not only as a player but also, and more importantly, as a person.

In the same way that Don Foutz's rushing led into the era of champions, Albert "Zuke" Zuchegno carried Dover out. Zuke played for the Tornadoes from 1933 to 1936, setting nearly all of the school's rushing and scoring records. During Zuchegno's four years on the gridiron, his teams compiled a record of 25-9-4. The year 1935 was probably Zuchegno's greatest, as he set a state record by scoring twenty-seven touchdowns and total of 179 points to lead Dover to an 8-2 record. Zuke's career records held up for sixty years,

Dover's Football team is seen practicing at the fairgrounds, circa 1935. Shown in the picture are Joe Contini (#71) and Albert Zuchegno (#77). *Courtesy of Dave Contini.*

and he still holds those for most points scored in a game, most touchdowns in a game and most kick returns for a touchdown in a career.

After high school, Zuchegno was recruited by both Ohio State and Notre Dame, but he opted to remain a Buckeye. At Ohio State he is said to have been the fastest man on the team.

1936: New Phila, 14; Dover, 13

Before they played on a snowy Thanksgiving Day in 1936, no one would have expected this game to make the list of the greatest games ever. New Philadelphia had a dynamite team with a stellar 8-1 record. It was led by captain and starting left guard Bill Kuenzli, left end Mike Emery and halfbacks Leonard "Diz" Simonetti and Harold Stempfly. The head coach of the Quakers was John Brickels. During his tenure as New Philadelphia's coach from 1932 to 1937, Brickels amassed an outstanding record of 45-14-1. This included an undefeated team in 1934 and one-loss teams in 1936 and 1937. During its undefeated campaign in 1934, Brickel's squad clobbered an overmatched Dover team 49-0.

Dover, on the other hand, struggled mightily in 1936, despite the return of its outstanding running back Albert Zuchegno. It would finish the year with

The 1936 New Philadelphia High School football team. *Courtesy of the Quaker Foundation.*

Two Decades of Outstanding Players

a disappointing record of 3-4-2 in nine games. The low point of the season was an 82–6 rout by Canton McKinley. One of the reasons for Dover's disappointing year was injury. Both of Dover's talented backs, Zuchegno and fullback Don Groh, missed time with injuries. In addition to the two backs, Dover was led by two-time captain and right tackle Rocco Polce and Coach Herman "Bup" Rearick. During his time at Dover, Rearick compiled a record of 51-13-4, with three ten-win seasons and two campaigns in which his team finished undefeated.

For many reasons, New Philadelphia was heavily favored that Thanksgiving afternoon. Rumors circulated through the community that the mill boys were asking for thirty or forty points before they would put down money on Dover's team.

A crowd of more than five thousand turned out that afternoon and watched the Crimsons shock the heavily favored Quakers. New Philadelphia's star running back, Leonard Simonetti, fumbled the opening kickoff, which was picked up by Zuchegno on the Quaker twenty-eight-yard line, putting the Crimsons in business. Dover drove to the New Philadelphia fourteen-yard line before it was stopped on third down when end Earl Trammell was tackled before he could bring in the pass. The rule on the field was pass interference, and Dover was awarded a first down. On the next play, Zuchegno broke free for a five-yard touchdown. Web Fox put the extra point through the uprights, and Dover led the Quakers 7–0.

New Philadelphia would threaten to tie the game later that quarter, but a fumble again ruined its drive at Dover's thirty-eight-yard line. The Quakers put the ball on the ground four times, undoubtedly costing them several scoring opportunities and setting up Dover's first touchdown.

Despite their two big mistakes, New Philadelphia got things going in the second period. Leonard Simonetti redeemed himself with a twenty-six-yard scamper that set up a Harold Stempfly five-yard touchdown. The ensuing extra point by Emery knotted the score at 7–7. Although Dover put together a good drive before half, it couldn't score, and the game remained all tied up going into intermission.

All year long, New Philadelphia was known as a second-half team, and in the third quarter the Quakers didn't disappoint their loyal fans. With only four minutes gone in the third, New Philadelphia struck quickly. Simonetti broke off two consecutive runs of twenty-three and twenty-five yards, respectively, to give the Red and Black a 13–7 lead. Emery's kick was again true, and New Philadelphia led 14–7.

New Phila's relief at taking the lead was short-lived, though, when Dover's star, Al Zuchegno, struck pay dirt. On the first play after the kickoff, Zuchegno broke off a spectacular run of sixty-five yards for the touchdown. Dancing through a maze of Quaker players, Zuchegno broke two tackles and planted one hand on the ground before regaining his balance and scoring in one of the rivalry's longest touchdown runs. Unfortunately for the Crimsons, the snap on the extra point was not as spectacular as Zuchegno's run. The botched snap forced Dover kicker and left tackle Wilbur Fox to run for the extra point. The try was unsuccessful, and New Philadelphia clung to a 14–13 lead.

Through much of the rest of the game, New Philadelphia played smart, defensive football. Many times it punted on second or third downs to pin the Dover team deep. This was especially important in the fourth quarter, when Dover gave the Quakers a real scare.

After taking over at its own forty-eight-yard line, Dover began what could have been the game-winning drive. After running the popular Statue of Liberty play twice in four downs, the Crimsons were threatening at New Phila's twenty-eight-yard line. The Statue of Liberty play was pioneered by Amos Alonzo Stagg. In the play, the quarterback drops back as if he's going to throw a pass. Gripping the ball with his non-throwing hand, he places it behind his back and pump-fakes a pass with his throwing hand. While he is pretending to pass the ball, a running back or wide receiver takes the ball from his non-throwing hand and runs in the opposite direction of the fake pass.

After the two successful trick plays, Dover's Don Groh electrified the Quaker Stadium crowd when he knifed his way through the New Phila defenders and appeared to score the go-ahead touchdown on a twenty-nine-yard run. The celebration was premature though, as on the play Dover was flagged for illegal motion by one of the other backs. The play was called back, and New Philadelphia still clung to its 14–13 lead. It was the third time that Dover was penalized for illegal motion in the game.

Although the drive continued all the way to the fourteen-yard line, a timely interception by Harold Stempfly ended the scoring threat. After the interception, New Philadelphia ran out the clock and celebrated victory over

Two Decades of Outstanding Players

its crosstown rivals. The star of the game for the victors was Simonetti, who accounted for 139 yards on eleven carries. He also did all of the team's punting and passing.

1937: Dover's Crater Stadium

One of the greatest things about the Dover-New Philadelphia rivalry is their proximity. Whenever one community is victorious or possesses something the other does not, there is jealousy. While this may be true of other not so close geographical rivals, competition is always greatest when the two are closer to each other. Unlike two separate communities, residents of Dover and New Phila are constantly traveling between the two towns, and as the old saying goes, familiarity breeds contempt.

As the 1920s bled into the 1930s and the Great Depression worsened, residents of Dover began clamoring for their own stadium, independent

An early photo of Dover's Crater Stadium. *Courtesy of Denny Rubright.*

of the county fairgrounds. New Philadelphia had constructed a beautiful stadium in 1928, adding lights two years later, and undoubtedly this discretion between the communities was a bur in the saddle of the Crimsons and their fans. So after almost ten years of having to hear about New Phila's beautiful new stadium, Dover's school board worked through Roosevelt's Works Progress Administration and secured the money to build a stadium that would rival the home field of the Quakers.

While residents may have been clamoring for a new stadium, the school board took notice after a conflict arose in the scheduling of the fairgrounds. This conflict forced the Crimsons to alter their schedule to accommodate the Tuscarawas County Fair. Once, during the 1934 season, the Crimson and Gray was even forced to play a home game at Quaker Stadium. Taking all of these factors into account, it was enough to motivate the board to begin planning a stadium of their own. The first step in this process was securing the land. This was accomplished when Dover resident Harry Crater and his sister, Leah Senhauser, of New Philadelphia agreed to donate a fourteen-acre parcel from the Crater Farm to the school district. The acreage was originally used as a sand pit and a rubbish dump but was perfect for a stadium.

Plans were made, and the stadium would be built for the sum of $98,329.99. The WPA would take care of all but $12,799.99 of that total, which would fall to the school district. In addition to the obvious boost to the local economy provided by the WPA, the stadium project also helped boost manufacturing with its order of 660,000 bricks. The Stone Creek Brick Company, which was awarded the contract, provided thirty days labor for seventy men just to fill the order.

Once the bricks arrived, work began on the stadium in the spring of 1937. The exterior wall of the stadium was made entirely of brick and was fashioned in the shape of a D. It took all summer to complete the work, and the stadium was finished only two days before the first scheduled game on September 18, 1937. That afternoon, the Crimsons defeated Akron Kenmore 19–7, with Don Groh scoring the stadium's first touchdown.

Over the years, many improvements have been made to the stadium, including the various scoreboards, locker rooms, concession stands and the band shell added in 1980. The most important addition, though, came only one year after the stadium was constructed. In 1938, stadium lights were added, putting Dover's stadium on par with its rival across the river.

Two Decades of Outstanding Players

1938–1940: Wayne "Woody" Hayes and the New Philadelphia Quakers

For a small rural farming community, the village of Newcomerstown has produced two incredibly important sports figures. It is hard to believe that both Denton "Cy" Young and Wayne "Woody" Hayes both grew up in such a small town. It is even harder to fathom that the two men were contemporaries and actually enjoyed a friendship.

Although Wayne Hayes was not born in rural Tuscarawas County, his formative years were spent there and his work ethic was cemented in the small town of Newcomerstown. Hayes was born in Noble County, the son of a hardworking teacher. His father instilled a never-say-die attitude in his son and a deep respect for education.

In 1920, when Woody was only seven, his father moved their young family to Tuscarawas County, where he took a job as Newcomerstown's

Pictured is one of the only images of Wayne "Woody" Hayes coaching the New Philadelphia Quakers. Hayes is in the background with the black fedora. *Courtesy of the Quaker Foundation.*

superintendant of schools. The young Hayes settled in nicely, making friends and earning a reputation as a bruiser. One of those new friends of Hayes was local legend Cy Young. Hayes spent time in the summer working at Young's farm and listening to the old legend tell stories of his playing days.

Although he was never an incredibly gifted athlete, Woody was tough, and he excelled at sports in high school. He played football, basketball and baseball, doing well enough that he was able to continue his football career while attending Denison University near Columbus. In addition to playing football, Woody carried a full slate of courses at the small private college. He double majored in history and English while achieving a minor in both Spanish and physical education.

After college, the young Hayes had two job offers, one to be an assistant football coach in Mingo Junction, Ohio, and another at a larger school to coach basketball. Even though the money was better at the larger school, Woody's love of football won out, and he accepted the position in Mingo Junction. Woody remained in his first job for only a year until opportunity came knocking. In the summer of 1936, Woody accepted a position as an assistant football coach at New Philadelphia.

Coming to New Philadelphia was a great decision for Hayes. The New Phila job provided him with a mentor who would help to shape his coaching philosophy. In the fall of 1936, the New Phila Quakers were led by head coach John Brickels. Between 1932 and 1937, Brickels compiled a record of 45-14-1; more importantly, he recommended Hayes as his successor in 1938, when he left the Quakers. This was Woody's first and only head coaching job at the high school level. Interestingly, the careers of Hayes and Brickels would intertwine again when both men worked together at Miami University in Oxford, Ohio. This time, though, Brickels would be in the role of athletic director, with Woody as his head football coach. In addition to his jobs with New Phila and Miami of Ohio, Brickels would serve as head basketball coach at West Virginia University and work for Paul Brown when he was the head coach of the Cleveland Browns.

When Brickels left to coach Huntington High School in West Virginia in 1938, Hayes was named the Quakers' new head coach. Woody was twenty-six years old. In his first two years as coach, Hayes's Quakers were outstanding. During the 1938 and 1939 seasons, his teams compiled a record of 18-1-1 with two wins over the rival Tornadoes. The 1939 season was

Two Decades of Outstanding Players

especially rewarding as the team posted an undefeated record and clobbered Dover 46–0.

Hayes's time at New Philadelphia was not all roses, though. For everything that went right during his first two years, everything went wrong in 1940. The young coach lost nearly every starter from his 1939 squad and became a victim of his own success. Despite his very inexperienced team, the community expected great things from the young coach with an 18-1-1 career mark. What the community didn't expect was a 1-9 record. Included in the dismal season was a 19–0 loss to the team's crosstown rival in what would be Hayes's last game.

Never a gracious loser, Woody's mood and behavior darkened with his team's struggles, and his behavior toward his young players turned increasingly harsh and profane. In response to Woody's outbursts and anger issues, some in the community began to criticize the coach. Possibly the biggest critic was Superintendant H.S. Carroll, who refused to recommend that Woody be retained for the 1941 season. Although Carroll would later change his tune after members of the New Phila community rallied behind Hayes, the damage was already done.

Woody would remain at New Phila through the 1940–41 school year and guide the Quakers through spring practice, but he would never again roam the sidelines of Quaker Stadium. In the summer of 1941, Woody Hayes enlisted in the navy and left the high school coaching ranks forever. Later, as a college coach, Hayes won 238 games. The bulk of these came at Ohio State, where he compiled a record of 205-61-10. He coached the Buckeyes for twenty-eight seasons.

1945: Dover, 6; New Phila, 0—The Final Game on Thanksgiving Day

Coming into their final Thanksgiving Day game on November 22, 1945, both Dover and New Phila shared similar records. Dover was 7-2 on the season, while New Philadelphia was slightly better at 7-1-1. Despite their similar records, New Philadelphia was the favorite. It was led by third-year head coach Paul Hoerneman and co-captains Bob McMillen and Eddie Warmack. During his three years at New Phila, Hoerneman compiled a

The Dover-Phila Football Rivalry

The 1945 Dover High School football team. *Courtesy of the Dover Historical Society.*

stellar record of 24-2-3. In addition, prior to that afternoon he had defeated the Crimsons in their two previous meetings.

Dover was led by legendary coach Glen "Dutch" Furbay. With a career record of 85-50-4, Furbay had the longest tenure as Dover coach until current coach, Dan Ifft, passed him in 2009. At the time, Furbay was in his fourth year coaching the Crimsons, with a record of 1-2 against the Phils. His only win came in 1942, his first year as coach, when his team put together a 10-0 season. While not a Dover alumni, Furbay was local, graduating from Uhrichsville before attending Muskingum College.

The Crimsons were led by captain and fullback Tommy Koledin and left halfback Dick Ellwood. Both men also played prominent roles on defense as linebackers. Coming into the rivalry game, Dover had won six in a row after starting the year 1-2.

The last Thanksgiving Day game between the rivals was played in frigid temperatures and hurricane-force winds at Crater Stadium in front of fifty-three hundred fans. In the game, Ellwood and Koledin accounted for all but twenty-one yards on offense, with Koledin scoring the game's lone touchdown. New Philadelphia showed very little life on offense in the first three quarters, managing no first downs. Almost all of its yards and all six first downs it managed came in the fourth quarter when it almost rallied past the home team.

Two Decades of Outstanding Players

The tone of the game appears to have been set early when Dover's punter, Ellwood, dropped back to punt from his own twenty-two-yard line in the first quarter. Kicking into the wind, the ball was booted off Ellwood's foot and sailed out of bounds for a net gain of only three yards. The Quakers took over with first and ten on Dover's twenty-five-yard line. Despite this early opportunity, New Philadelphia managed to gain only five yards before turning over the ball on downs. It was quickly apparent that the fans that afternoon were to witness a defensive struggle.

Dover's first scoring opportunity went only slightly better than that of the Quakers. Early in the second quarter, Dover's linebacker Tommy Koledin broke through and blocked an Eddie Warmack punt, giving Dover possession at the New Philadelphia thirty-two-yard line. Two quick plays and the Tornadoes looked to be in business. After a six-yard run by Koledin and a twenty-yarder by Ellwood, Dover had first and ten at the New Phila six. It wasn't meant to be, though, as Koledin fumbled on the half-yard line and the Quaker's recovered to end the threat.

Even with the disappointment of this lost opportunity to overcome, Dover was quickly back in scoring position. After holding the Quakers deep in their own territory, Eddie Warmack got off a beautiful punt that sailed all the way to the forty-one-yard line. It was returned by Dover's right halfback, Buddy Truman, who worked a little magic of his own, picking up thirteen yards. Dover was again in business with a first and ten at New Phila's thirty-yard line.

This time, Dover didn't let its opportunity get away. On fourth and one, Dick Ellwood broke loose, sweeping the ball around the right end for a ten-yard gain and a first and ten at New Philadelphia's twelve-yard line. From there, the stunned Quakers were treated to a strong dose of fullback Tommy Koledin, who carried the ball on three consecutive plays, punching it in from the one-yard line for the game's only score. On the extra point attempt, Quaker captain Bob McMillen rallied his team, blocking the extra point to keep the score a very tight 6–0.

Neither team did much through the rest of the second period and into the third. Dover did move the ball a little; its most successful drive in the second half stalled at the twenty-one-yard line.

Finally, in the fourth quarter New Philadelphia seemed to wake up. After a booming sixty-yard punt by Ellwood, with the wind, to end the third quarter,

New Philadelphia started to move the ball. Beginning at its own twenty-yard line, three successful passes to fullback Burton Beaber and halfbacks Yaggi and Stephens took the ball out to the thirty-six. On the next two plays, New Philadelphia went for it all and just missed. Both long passes were incomplete, and Dover took over on downs. As the *Daily Reporter* noted after the game, "Either one of which was a sure touchdown."

With time running out, the two teams went back and forth before New Philadelphia took over for one last, desperate drive. Beginning at Dover's thirty-five, the Quakers faced a fourth down with less than a minute to play. An exciting nine-yard run gave New Philadelphia a first down with only a few seconds remaining on the clock. With time running out, fullback Beaber dropped back to pass and heaved one over the middle to the Quaker left end, Phipps, who was dragged down as time expired. In a finish reminiscent of Super Bowl XXIV between the St. Louis Rams and the Tennessee Titans, New Phila lost the game inside the ten as time expired.

On a side note, New Phila's Burton Beaber showed incredible courage playing the entire game with a badly bruised and lacerated hand. Even with the injury, which occurred in the first quarter, Beaber nearly won the game for the Quakers.

1946: New Phila, 3; Dover, 0

When two teams play each other for over one hundred years, you would think there would be a good number of upsets. Surprisingly, this isn't true in the case of the Dover-Phila rivalry. Very rarely in the history of the series has one team come in the clear underdog and left the field as the victor. The year 1946 is an exception to this rule.

Coming into the big game, no one gave New Philadelphia a chance. In his column "Right Down the Line," future *Times Reporter* editor Harry Yockey picked the Tornadoes to win 33–0. It's rumored that local gamblers were giving twenty-six points to anyone willing to bet on the county-seaters. To understand the reasoning behind these bold predictions, you need to look no further than the two teams' records and common opponents. Coming into the game, New Phila had a dismal 2-7 record, while Dover sported a much better mark at 6-2-1. As far as common opponents, the

Two Decades of Outstanding Players

The 1946 New Philadelphia High School football team. *Courtesy of the Quaker Foundation.*

two teams shared two. Dover defeated Coshocton (18–0) and Uhrichsville (13–0), while New Phila lost to Coshocton (7–0) and was blown out by the Uhrichsville Tigers (32–0).

Looking deeper than records, on paper Dover had the superior team led by star player Dick Ellwood. Coming into the Dover-Phila game, Ellwood had scored twenty touchdowns for 120 points. By comparison, New Philadelphia's entire team had scored only 58 points coming into the big game. In addition to Ellwood, Dover's starting eleven featured nine seniors and a twenty-year-old sophomore in their final game for their alma mater. The twenty-year-old sophomore was Homer Rinehart, who had returned to school after serving his country in World War II.

New Philadelphia was led by Carlton "Shorty" Long and Orval Stephens. The two seniors accounted for thirty-seven of the team's fifty-eight points. Coaching the underdog Quakers was Syl Harmon in his only year at New Phila. Harmon was assisted by a young coach named William "Bill" Kidd. After Harmon's departure, Kidd would take over the head-coaching duties and lead the Red and Black for the next fourteen years. In the process, Kidd would come to be known as New Philadelphia's greatest coach, compiling a career record at New Phila of 82-48-8.

The Dover-Phila Football Rivalry

As festivities kicked off the week of the big game, both communities planned bonfires and snake dances through their respective downtowns. One difference in the pre-game activities was a special addition to Dover's bonfire. The previous evening, someone cut the fence to gain access into Quaker Stadium and then proceeded to steal the crossbar from the goal post. Miraculously, this crossbar then turned up atop the Tornadoes' bonfire. While there had been several examples of vandalism following the big game, this is one of the first examples of vandalism before the game. In addition to the incident with Dover's bonfire, two young women from New Philadelphia were caught red-handed. Their red hands came from the red paint they were using to paint "NP" in front of Dover High School.

When the day of the big game finally arrived, Dover traveled to New Philadelphia to take on the underdog Quakers. The day itself was cold with a stiff wind. Whether it was the weather or the dire predictions for the home team, the attendance at the 1946 game was well below average. Fewer than thirty-five hundred tickets were sold for the game. At one point, New Philadelphia was even forced to ship several hundred tickets to Dover, as it was unable to sell them to its hometown fans.

From the opening quarter, it became clear that the game would be a defensive battle. Dover moved the ball a little in the first quarter, but costly turnovers ended any attempts to score. In the end, it would be the multitude of turnovers that would come back to haunt the heavily favored Tornadoes. Things started poorly for the home team as well, as it lost one of its two stars, Shorty Long, in the very first period of play.

The situation appeared to go from bad to worse in the second period when New Phila fullback Ted Demattio was called for clipping on a punt return. Already deep in their own territory, Demattio's mental misstep pushed the Quakers all the way back to their own six. This virtually assured the Tornadoes a shot at good field position before the end of the first half. Another penalty pushed the Quakers back to their one before Bud Williams saved the day by getting off a good punt. Williams would be one of New Philadelphia's most important cogs that afternoon, averaging an outstanding thirty-six yards per punt on fourteen punts.

Even with Williams's great punt, a short Dover return still gave it first and ten at the Quaker forty-nine. On third down, as Ellwood faded back to pass, Demattio redeemed himself and made the first big play of a very big day

Two Decades of Outstanding Players

as the Quaker junior intercepted Ellwood's pass and raced across midfield. Thirty yards later, the Tornadoes brought him down, but New Philadelphia had its first scoring opportunity of the game.

On the very next play, Demattio completed a pass, New Phila's only completion of the game, to right end Bernard Heaton. Heaton took the ball down to Dover's twenty-yard line, setting up a first and ten with less than a minute left on the clock. After two incomplete passes, New Phila's coach Syl Harmon elected to try something that the Quakers hadn't done all season. Harmon sent Paul Miskimen onto the field to try a twenty-three-yard field goal.

With Demattio lining up to hold, Miskimen positioned himself for the kick. Fighting a stiff wind, the inexperienced kicker connected cleanly with the ball and watched it sail just over the crossbar to give New Philadelphia the lead. Only thirty-five seconds remained in the half. The field goal was the only one of Miskimen's career.

As the teams headed into their respective locker rooms, both bands performed for the crowd at Quaker Stadium. Dover decided to debut a new routine that would prove rather embarrassing in light of the eventual outcome of the game. The Tornado band began by forming both a capital D and a capital P. The P then dissolved, only to be reformed inside a large D. The climax of the routine was when those making up the P removed white handkerchiefs and waved them to the crowd while the announcer bragged, "New Philadelphia surrenders to Dover." Unfortunately for the Crimson and Gray, that was the only victory it would have that afternoon.

Although the second half was dominated by Dover, neither team managed a score. In the final period alone, Dover threatened three times but in all three came up empty. The biggest disappointment for the Tornadoes came after a long pass by Ellwood. Ellwood threw to left end Dick Mathias for a forty-six-yard gain, only to be stymied by Ted Demattio again. As Mathias broke loose, it looked as though he would go all the way for the game-winning score, but Demattio came out of nowhere to catch him at the fourteen-yard line. A costly fumble on the next play pushed Dover back eleven yards, and two plays later the Tornadoes turned over the ball on downs at the New Phila twenty. The fumble was one of five that afternoon for the Tornadoes, along with two interceptions. Although they were able to recover three of their fumbles, the Tornadoes had four turnovers in the game while New Philadelphia had none.

Dover's last gasp came on a fourth and one deep in New Phila territory with the game winding down in the fourth quarter. Instead of the obvious play, which would've been an Ellwood run, Dover coach Glen Furbay instead called for Ellwood to throw the ball. In the final of his heroics that afternoon, Demattio knocked the pass incomplete to preserve the victory for the Phils.

1949: THE BATTLE OF THE BAT

It all started with a bonfire speech. Coming into the big matchup with its crosstown rivals in 1949, Dover held its annual bonfire. One of the common themes that year was the idea that even with a 4-4 record, the Tornadoes were destined to defeat their rivals because their strength of schedule was much tougher than that of the Quakers. Dover played in the Central Ohio League with powerhouses like Newark, Lancaster, Zanesville and Chillicothe, while New Philadelphia played in the weaker Eastern Ohio Scholastic League with teams like East Liverpool and Canton Timken.

Playing on this theme, L.H. Alexander, Dover's legendary band director and composer of the school's fight song and alma mater, called out New Philadelphia for playing inferior talent. At Dover's bonfire on November 18, 1949, Alexander exclaimed, "New Philadelphia has been playing in the minor leagues all year, but on Friday night they will step up into the major leagues when they meet the Dover Tornadoes." Unfortunately, the Quakers didn't share the sentiment as they went out the following evening and clobbered Dover 27–6.

The concept of a major-league and a minor-league team would have ended there if it were not for a letter to *Daily Reporter* sportswriter Rex Ridenour. A few weeks after the end of the season, Ridenour published a letter from Harold Kennedy concerning a trophy for the winner of the big game. Kennedy was a Dover resident and member of the Tornado Club, but with roots in New Philadelphia. In his letter, Kennedy proposed that two bats be created, one for the major-league team and another for the minor leaguers. The winner of the game would take home the big bat, and the loser would be stuck with the minor-league version.

Kennedy's idea was then picked up by the Tornado club, which decided to make only one major-league bat that would serve as a trophy to be taken

Two Decades of Outstanding Players

home and displayed by the winning team every year. No one knows for sure whether the first bat was custom made or simply selected at a sporting goods store, but what we do know is that the thirty-nine-inch ash bat received a special touch at the hands of Dover's master carver Mooney Warther. The original bat features walnut and ivory inlays, including an inlayed football. The inlays form the words "Dover, New Philadelphia, Rotating, Football Trophy, Annual Award." Adjacent to the inlays are the words "Major League Champions" in ivory.

The bat's first public appearance was at the annual Tornado Club banquet in April 1950. The featured guest that evening was New Philadelphia coach William "Bill" Kidd, who was presented with the trophy. His presenter was none other than Dover band director L.H. Alexander, whose bonfire bravado resulted in the creation of the bat in the first place. In a lighthearted moment, Alexander handed the bat to Kidd as he said, "You may use this bat on anyone you please, but don't beat our brains out with it next November."

Kidd politely accepted the trophy and took a quick jab at Alexander by proclaiming that New Philadelphia was "proud to be a member of the Major Leagues." This was the last time that Alexander and the Tornadoes would see the major-league trophy for quite some time. New Philadelphia remained the major-league team for the next five years. Dover didn't win the "Battle of the Bat" until a 34–20 victory secured the trophy in 1955.

As the decades passed, the bat has continued to shuffle back and forth between the schools but has lost some of its luster. This is partially due to the fact that scores in the 1980s and 1990s were engraved smaller and smaller due to the rapidly diminishing space. That changed, though, in 1998, when Dover alumni Doug Klar and Dover football aficionado Denny Rubright decided to look into the possibility of a new bat.

The idea came when Klar took the bat to Warther's Museum to have that year's score engraved. The idea was hatched of having a new bat made to celebrate the fiftieth anniversary of the tradition. The Warther family agreed, and work began on a new bat. Mooney Warther's grandchildren, Carol, Dan and Dale, all worked on the new bat, with Dale adding the finishing touches and inlays. The new bat even included an inlaid football similar to the one that graced the barrel of the original. With a little luck, the new bat will carry on the tradition for another fifty years.

3
AN ERA OF CHANGE
1950–1969

1947–1960: NEW PHILADELPHIA COACH WILLIAM "BILL" KIDD

To coach Bill Kidd, it must have felt like he would never get his chance. Prior to being named New Phila's grid coach in 1947, Kidd served as an assistant for thirteen seasons. At New Phila alone, Kidd was an assistant under three other head coaches. In the end, Kidd's patience finally paid off. When he got his shot in 1947, he didn't disappoint. Bill Kidd went on to become New Philadelphia's winningest football coach.

William Kidd was born in Gahanna, Ohio, where he graduated in 1928. As a high school football player, he was good enough to continue his playing days at Capital University. Playing on the Capital team, Kidd's leadership abilities blossomed, and he was named team captain during his senior season in 1932.

Following college, Bill Kidd began to work at his coaching resume. He had a short stint at Jeffersonville as an assistant before moving on to St. Clairsville, where he spent six seasons. In addition to his duties as assistant football coach, Kidd also headed up the baseball, basketball and golf teams.

In 1942, Kidd decided to leave St. Clairsville, moving to New Philadelphia, where he became the junior high football coach working on the staff of Stanley Plummer. In his two years at New Phila, Plummer went 4-5 in 1941 and 2-8 in 1942. After the 1942 season, he stepped down and was replaced by coach Paul Hoerneman, a 1934 graduate of New Phila.

Hoerneman was an outstanding coach, and a young Bill Kidd learned a great deal working on his staff. In three years at New Phila, Hoerneman compiled a record of 24-3-3. Despite his success on the football field, Hoerneman was actually better known for his prowess as a basketball coach. In eight seasons with the Quakers, Hoerneman led the New Phila cagers to a 144-33 record and a State Championship during the 1939–40 season. In 1946, Hoerneman left New Philadelphia to return to his college alma mater, where he took over as the head coach of both the basketball and football teams.

New Philadelphia coach William "Bill" Kidd.
Courtesy of Denny Rubright.

After Hoerneman resigned, Kidd was again retained as an assistant with yet another head coach. In 1946, New Philadelphia hired Syl Harmon to lead its squad. Harmon lasted only one season before making the decision to step back and coach the junior high team instead of the varsity. With Harmon's resignation, Bill Kidd finally got his chance at the big job.

Hired in 1947 to replace Harmon, Kidd would remain the face of the New Philadelphia Quakers for the next fourteen seasons. While the team struggled to a 4-4-1 record in 1947, the tide was turning. Over the next four years, Kidd put together a streak of four consecutive winning seasons and a record of 34-5-1. More importantly, Kidd won four consecutive years against the rival Tornadoes. By the time Kidd stepped down in 1960, his career record stood at 82-48-8, including undefeated teams in 1950 and 1953. His eighty-two wins are the most of any Quaker coach in the program's history.

More importantly than wins and losses is the work that Kidd did to develop some of New Philadelphia's greatest players. Among those who played for

An Era of Change

Bill Kidd are Jim Metcalf, Jerry Wampfler, Sam Miller, Ed Breehl, Nick Scalambrino, Jim Massarelli, Bill "Cannonball" Cooper and 1955 Rose Bowl MVP Dave Leggett.

Against Dover, Kidd was outstanding, with a record of 9-4-1. Under his guidance, the Quakers dominated the series during the 1950s, losing only twice to the Tornadoes in a ten-year stretch from 1950 to 1959. Included in the Quaker's domination was the largest defeat in the history of the rivalry, a 72–0 shellacking in 1956.

In December 1960, Bill Kidd made the difficult decision to step down as Quaker coach. He was replaced by Al Christopher. After his career was over, Kidd was honored by numerous Halls of Fame, including the Ohio High School Football Coaches Association Hall of Fame, the National High School Hall of Fame and the Capital University Varsity C Hall of Fame.

1950: New Phila, 19; Dover, 12

The early 1950s were good to the New Philadelphia Quakers. Under the guidance of coach William "Bill" Kidd, they would compile a record of 54-21-4 between 1948 and 1957. They would also produce some of their greatest players during this era and post the worst blowout in the history of the Dover-Phila rivalry in 1956. By the time the decade ended, New Philadelphia could brag of seven wins to only two for its crosstown rivals with one tie. New Phila's decade of dominance had to start somewhere, which brings us back to a great game in 1950.

Coming into the showdown in 1950, both teams had put together good records. Dover stood at 8-1, with its only loss coming the previous week against Zanesville, while New Philadelphia was 8-0-1, with a lone tie against Bellaire. On the sidelines, the Quakers were again led by Bill Kidd. Kidd had won two straight against the Tornadoes and looked to make it three in 1951. Dover continued to be led by head coach Glen "Dutch" Furbay in his ninth year at Dover. Although his overall record of 85-50-4 was outstanding, Furbay always seemed to struggle with Phila during his fourteen-year coaching tenure at Dover. From 1942 to 1955, he went 4-9-1.

Leading the Quaker charge in 1950 were two outstanding players, William "Dave" Leggett and Richard "Dick" Stephenson. Stephenson

New Philadelphia quarterback Dave Leggett pictured as an Ohio State Buckeye. Leggett led Ohio State to the 1954 National Championship and was named the MVP of the 1955 Rose Bowl. *Courtesy of the Quaker Foundation.*

played center and linebacker on New Philadelphia's team and would go on to play at Muskingum College. After college, Dick Stephenson went on to law school at the Ohio State University. He later returned to New Philadelphia and has become a leader in the community.

Quarterback Dave Leggett is one of the greatest players ever to don the Red and Black. While a Quaker, Leggett led the state-ranked football and basketball teams. He was co-captain of both. As a member of the basketball team, he set the state single season scoring record. After his career at New Phila, Leggett attended the Ohio State University. As a junior, Leggett broke into the starting lineup. Later, he led the Buckeyes to victory in the 1955 Rose Bowl, earning MVP honors.

After his graduation from Ohio State, Leggett played professional football and served his country as a member of the U.S. Air Force. During his professional career, he played for the Chicago Cardinals, Saskatchewan Rough Riders and as a player/coach in the European Military Football League. After his playing days were over, Leggett went on to coach at the U.S. Air Force Academy from 1967 to 1971.

While New Philadelphia had an outstanding team, Dover was no slouch. It came into the rivalry game with an excellent record of 8-1, with its only loss coming against Zanesville. For the first nine games of the season, Dover's offense was led by quarterback Frank Ellwood. Only a sophomore, Ellwood was already in his second year as the team's starting quarterback. As a freshman, he threw seven touchdown passes. In the first nine games of 1950, he threw nine more. In addition to his strong arm, Ellwood also served as the team's kicker beginning his freshman year. Unfortunately for the Tornadoes, Ellwood was unavailable for the 1950 game, as he was injured the previous week. Instead, Dover was led by senior backup quarterback Merwin Yockey.

The 1950 game was played on November 17 in good weather and featured a last-minute broadcast and a special sideline guest. The special guest was none other than Miami University head coach Wayne "Woody" Hayes. As coach from 1938 to 1940, Hayes led the Quakers to a 19-10-1 record and two wins over the archrival Tornadoes. In addition to Woody Hayes, the Quakers had another addition to their sidelines. For the first time in the history of the rivalry, they were joined by a broadcast team from local radio station WJER.

In a last-minute decision, the New Philadelphia athletic board voted to allow the radio station to broadcast the game. Without proper prep time, WJER found that its equipment was less than adequate for the broadcast. The main problem was that the cords were too short to reach the press box. The station was forced to improvise, and the broadcasters called the game from the cinder track just behind New Philadelphia's bench. Even if they'd had cords long enough to reach the box, it's doubtful they would have had room to broadcast. The press box in those days was barely big enough to accommodate the timer, press and public address announcer.

Beginning with the opening kickoff that evening at Quaker Stadium, the Red and Black came out hot. It took the kickoff at its own thirty-six and drove straight down the field for its first score. The big play of the opening drive was a nineteen-yard pass from Phila quarterback Dave Leggett to halfback Bill Richards. Richards then put the Phils in front with a four-yard plunge over right tackle.

At the end of the first quarter, the Quakers were again in business after a Dover fumble at their own forty-five-yard line. This was one of three Dover fumbles in the first half, two of which were converted into Quaker touchdowns. After the fumble, the Quakers were again led downfield by Leggett, who handed off to fullback Sammy Miller. Miller broke through for a touchdown and a 13–0 lead with just a few seconds gone in the second period.

After a series of turnovers by both squads ping-ponged possession back and forth, New Philadelphia found itself with the ball on its own thirty-yard line with just a few minutes remaining in the second quarter. The time remaining was just enough as the Phils marched seventy yards in nine plays to take a commanding 19–0 lead into halftime against the helpless Tornadoes. The touchdown came as the final seconds ticked off the clock on a nine-yard run by Leggett.

While Dover had been dominated by a superior Quaker squad in the first half, it came out a different team in the third quarter. Beginning with the second half kickoff, Dover put together an epic drive. After returning the kickoff to their own twenty-five-yard line, the Tornadoes laced together a twenty-six-play, ten-and-a-half-minute drive that ate up almost the entire third quarter. In that one drive alone, they converted on fourth down three times, the final time on fourth and goal. The final conversion gave the Crimson Tornados their first score on a one-yard plunge by halfback Al Evans. In addition to the scoring drive, New Philadelphia was further set back when its quarterback, Leggett, had to leave the game due to a broken nose.

As the third quarter faded into the fourth, Dover was again in business after a punt by the Quakers gave them first down and ten at their own forty-two-yard line. This time, it wouldn't take an epic double-digit play drive to reach the end zone. Dover scored on a trick play just five plays later to get back in the game. On the scoring play, quarterback Merwin Yockey pitched to halfback Al Evans, who pulled up for a halfback pass. The ball was caught downfield by right end Carl Barlock, who took it in from the twenty for the score. With only a few minutes remaining in the game, Dover was down only 19–12.

The next possession by the Quakers went nowhere, and Dover had a shot to take the lead with only a few minutes remaining in the fourth quarter. Again, Dover pushed its luck with a fourth and one. This time, the New Phila defense was up to the task. It stopped the Tornadoes and had only to run out the remaining few minutes of the game to hold on for the win. This was easier said than done, though, as the Phils had proven utterly incapable of moving the ball during the second half. What Phila needed to secure the game was a boost. That's exactly what it got.

With only a few minutes separating it from victory, a shocked crowd watched as the injured New Phila quarterback Dave Leggett ran onto the field. Leggett calmed the jittery New Philadelphia offense, leading it on the drive it needed to clinch the game. Dover's offense wouldn't get another chance as time ran out with New Phila on Dover's sixteen-yard line, securing the 19–12 victory.

An Era of Change

1955: Dover, 34; New Phila, 20

With the exception of the 1956 and 1998 games that are to follow, no game in this book features a larger point spread than the 1955 game. Unlike the 1956 game, which represents the worst drubbing in the history of the rivalry, the game that follows was a lot better game than the final score shows. It was also an important game for all the intangibles not played out on the field.

Although no one knew it at the time, 1955 would be the last season for Dover's legendary coach Glen "Dutch" Furbay. Furbay was the Tornadoes coach from 1942 to 1955, compiling a record of 85-50-4 for Dover over fourteen seasons. Only one man has coached Dover longer—current coach Dan Ifft—and only two have more wins than Furbay, Ifft and Dick Haines. Despite his many accomplishments, Furbay never seemed to have much luck against his crosstown rival. In his fourteen seasons, the Tornadoes managed only four wins and one tie against New Phila. To make things worse, against New Phila's outstanding coach Bill Kidd, Furbay managed only two wins in nine tries, with one tie. Fortunately for Furbay, one of those wins was in his final year of 1955.

The 1955 Dover High School football team. *Courtesy of Denny Rubright.*

The Dover-Phila Football Rivalry

Coming into the big game that year, neither team had enjoyed a successful season. Both Furbay's Tornadoes and Kidd's Quakers were a disappointing 4-5. Throughout the year, both teams were haunted by injuries to key players. Coming into the big game, both were relatively healthy, with the lone exception being Dover's Jim Heller, who was a late scratch due to an intestinal flu that had him hospitalized.

Dover was led in 1955 by co-captains Burt Link and Dewey Grafe. Dover's backfield was loaded that year with Link, a two-hundred-pound fullback, Grafe at halfback and, at the other halfback position, speedy "Jumpin" Joe Lowery. Lowery's speed carried him to the team's lead in touchdowns scored, with seven.

The New Phila Quakers were led by co-captains Bob Gilmore and Bob Huff. On offense, the fighting Phils featured end Dave Seabrook as the leading scorer, with seven touchdowns, followed closely by Bill Carpenter, with six.

In addition to bragging rights for a year, the game also offered Dover a chance to acquire the coveted major-league bat for the first time since its inception in 1949.

As the first kickoff sailed through the night in the fifty-first game between the two rivals, Dover didn't waste any time. Dover's Ronnie Rothacher recovered a New Phila fumble on the Dover forty-four-yard line on Phila's first drive. Only one play later, Joe Lowery broke off a beautiful run that culminated fifty-six yards later with the Tornadoes' first score of the game. Only four minutes had ticked off the clock.

Lightning struck a second time for the Tornadoes at the end of the first quarter when Lowery broke off a near identical run. From his own forty-one, on the first play of the drive, Lowery scampered fifty-nine yards for his second touchdown of the game. After a missed extra point, Dover led 13–0 at the end of the first frame.

The two teams went back and forth for most of the second quarter before a costly turnover allowed the Quakers to get on the board. A Dover fumble at its own forty-seven with only a minute left in the half put New Phila into its hurry-up offense. Hurry up would accurately describe the Phila scoring drive. On first down, quarterback Jim Rolli threw to end Bill "Cannonball" Cooper, who hauled in the pass and ran all the way to the Dover fourteen-yard line for a thirty-nine-yard gain. On the very next play,

An Era of Change

Rolli was at it again as Bill Carpenter hauled in a touchdown pass in the corner of the end zone.

The score remained 13–7 well into the third quarter before Dover was able to put together another good drive. Taking over at their own thirty-six-yard line, Burt Link and Lowery carried the offense to midfield before Link got loose on a big gainer. Link rumbled forty-two yards to the ten before he was brought down by a Phila defender. The Quakers wouldn't be so lucky on the next play, though, as Link crossed the stripe for a ten-yard touchdown.

One common theme throughout the night was the Quakers' aerial attack, and on the next drive, it again produced a quick score. Jim Rolli got to work with a thirty-seven-yard strike to Cooper, followed by a forty-two-yard throw to end Ward Holdsworth. Again the Quakers scored, reducing the Dover lead to one score at 20–13.

With only fifty-five seconds left in the third frame, one would assume that the score would remain 20–13 going into the final quarter. However, one would be wrong. In yet another quick score, the Phila kickoff was returned by fullback Burt Link, who took it to the house. His seventy-seven-yard return was the perfect answer to New Phila's short-lived momentum. With only one quarter remaining, Dover led 27–13.

Surprisingly, the first half of the fourth quarter saw no scoring. Instead, both teams traded the ball back and forth. Midway through the fourth, the scoring picked up again as New Philadelphia put together a sustained drive starting at its own forty-six. The capper was a six-yard run by New Phila's Dave Seabrook that put the Quakers within a score of their rivals, at 27–20.

With six and a half minutes left, the teams traded possessions before the Quakers were pinned deep in their own territory by a good punt by the Tornadoes. In what was to be his last shot that afternoon, Jim Rolli stepped under center at the nine-yard line with dreams of leading a ninety-one-yard game-winning drive. Unfortunately for Rolli and the Quaker faithful, it wasn't to be. On first down, Rolli scrambled and fumbled. The ball was covered by Dover's Joe Demaree at the twelve, setting up the Tornadoes' final score.

Although Phila did get possession back one more time, it was unable to move the ball. Taking over on downs, Dover ran out the clock. The Dover victory that night was one of only two it would enjoy in a decade thoroughly dominated by the Red and Black. It was especially sweet the following spring when Glen "Dutch" Furbay announced that his coaching days were over.

The Dover-Phila Football Rivalry

1956: New Phila, 72; Dover, 0

If you are a fan of the Dover Tornadoes, please quit reading this now. The 1956 Dover-Phila game was the worst moment in Dover's football history. On the flip side, it remains a high-water mark for the Quaker program, which dominated the first fifty-plus years that the two teams played.

Although the Quakers were favored in 1956 pretty heavily, no one saw this coming. Odds makers were giving three touchdowns to the Crimson Tornadoes, not twelve. Believe it or not, local reporter Jim De Mello even picked the Tornadoes to win the contest, upsetting the Quakers 26–20.

To understand how 1956 happened, you have to take a closer look at the two teams coming into the big game. Dover that year was led by quarterback Charles Davis and halfbacks Ron Rothacher and Jim Heller. Gone were the two great players who led the Tornadoes to victory in 1955, Joe Lowery and Burt Link. In addition to the loss of its star players from the previous year, Dover was also plagued with injuries most of the season. At one point or another, most of its backfield missed at least one game. To further complicate these challenges was the presence of a new leader in coach Bill Kenny. Coach Kenny was twenty-five years old when

The 1956 New Philadelphia High School football team. *Courtesy of Denny Rubright.*

An Era of Change

he accepted the post. Prior to coming to Dover, he was a star player at Washington and Jefferson and a coach at Oberlin High School. He earned the nod after taking his perennially bad Oberlin squad to a 4-2-2 record in 1955. Kenny's tenure would last only two years at Dover as he put together a dismal 5-14 record.

Even with its struggles with injuries, a new coach and a new system, Dover still got off to a hot start that year beginning 3-0. It scored fifty-five points against Uhrichsville and thirty-nine against Chillicothe. These were the high points of the season as later the wheels fell off the offense. In the final six games of the season, Dover managed a total of only twenty points. Coming into the rivalry game, they were riding a six-game losing streak and had been crushed by Zanesville 53–0 in week nine.

In everything that Dover struggled with, New Philadelphia's team was as solid as a rock. Under coach Bill Kidd, in his tenth year, the Quakers were 7-1-1 coming into the big game. They were led by a slew of upperclassmen, including their outstanding quarterback Jim Rolli and fullback Bill "Cannonball" Cooper. Prior to the 1956 season, Coach Kidd had wisely made the decision to move the powerful Cooper to the fullback position. He had played end in 1955. At fullback, the two-hundred-pound Cooper was a man among boys. In 1956, he racked up 1,028 yards on 104 carries for an average of 9.8 yards per carry. He also crossed the goal line twelve times for the Red and Black.

Jim Rolli returned as a junior to start his second rivalry game, and Ward Holdsworth, who played end and scored in the 1955 game, was moved to center, where he anchored the line. With these strong core players, the Quakers averaged thirty points per game on offense.

In the week leading up to the big game, New Philadelphia focused on a solitary theme: revenge. Many of the Quaker players felt embarrassed to have lost to the Tornadoes the previous year, snapping a seven-year unbeaten streak. Coach Bill Kidd also seems to have latched onto this theme. At an Elks banquet the week of the game, Kidd gave one indication of how he would play it that Friday. When he was asked about substitutions, he said, "The game against Dover is dedicated to the seniors and the varsity. There will be no unnecessary substitutions."

At kickoff, over seven thousand fans were packed into Quaker Stadium. Things went badly for Dover from the start as it fumbled the opening kickoff.

Although they would hold the Quakers that drive, it would be about the only time that night that the Tornadoes were successful. On New Phila's second drive of the game, quarterback Jim Rolli took the ball in, from the two, kicking off the scoring barrage for the Quakers.

Offensively, New Phila rolled all night, and its stats are gaudy. It rolled up 513 yards of total offense, with 303 coming on the ground and another 210 through the air. The two quarterbacks that night, Rolli and Jim Watson, threw for three touchdowns, two of which were caught by sophomore Frank Fabiano. Rolli also ran for two scores. Despite his promise to keep the varsity in, Kidd did remove Rolli from the game at the end of the third quarter, allowing Watson to see some action.

While the quarterback numbers may be impressive, they pale in comparison to the statistics of "Cannonball" Cooper. Cooper rushed for 187 yards in the game on only eleven carries. In addition, he scored four touchdowns. Cooper's touchdowns helped New Phila to score in all four quarters, putting up nineteen points in the first, thirteen in the second, nineteen in the third and twenty-one in the final period. When he was asked about the score after the game, Bill Kidd told reporters, "I am sure that, if the situation were reversed, Dover would do likewise."

Just as impressive as New Philadelphia's dominance on offense was the show it put on with its defense. Dover managed only twenty-eight total yards on offense, fourteen on the ground and fourteen through the air. Dover's quarterbacks that evening had one completion in sixteen attempts. That lone completion to Ray Altier for fourteen yards gave it one of its only first downs. Probably the most impressive stat is that Dover never managed to cross midfield in the game. The closest it came was a drive that got it to its own forty-six before a fumble lost possession.

While this game is one that Dover fans would certainly like to forget, its inclusion in this book is important. It's important because it is such an anomaly. The vast majority of games between Dover and New Phila have been close. In all, 67 of the 107 games have been decided by fourteen points or less. Whether for better (in the case of the Quakers) or worse (for the Crimson Tornadoes), 1956 was certainly a memorable game.

An Era of Change

1958–1969: Dover Coach Dick Haines

Before Coach Dan Ifft obliterated all of Dover's coaching records, there was Dick Haines. Haines was the Tornado mentor for twelve seasons, forever changing the tide of the program and turning a good program and tradition into a great one.

Coach Haines was born in West Virginia, where he attended high school and later college. It was during his college career at West Liberty that Haines first exhibited the evidence of his great leadership ability. In his four years at the college, Coach Haines learned to win, which was something West Liberty did quite often during his time there. From 1947 to 1950, West Liberty put together an incredibly successful run, going 34-1-1. During much of this time, the team was led by Haines at quarterback anchoring the single-wing offense.

The winning continued as Haines coached tiny Adena High School and Triadelphia High School before settling in at Cadiz in 1956. During his two years serving as the Cadiz head football coach, the team went 8-0-1 and 7-2-

Dover coach Dick Haines and assistants Steve Kocheran and Jim Miller pictured during the 1959 season. *Courtesy of Denny Rubright.*

1, respectively. Building on this success, Haines jumped at the opportunity to move to Tuscarawas County in 1958.

Although his first year with the program was difficult—the team had a record of 4-5-1—Haines believed in his system and methods. In 1958, he inherited a team that had graduated most of its talent. Looking to build for the future, Haines played many of his juniors that year so that they could gain valuable experience. The plan worked, and in 1959, that same group of young men put together an 8-1-1 record for their thirty-three-year-old coach. More importantly, they scored a win over crosstown rival New Philadelphia.

The 1959 game was a breakthrough for the Tornadoes over the tradition-rich New Phila squad. Only four years earlier, when the seniors were freshman, they had watched a helpless Dover team get trounced 72–0. Now just a few short years later, they were handing out a beating of their own. In that memorable 1959 game—memorable, that is, if you are a Dover fan—the Tornadoes managed to score on the very first offensive play of the game. Jim Render passed to sophomore Jerry Bryan for a sixty-three-yard touchdown. From there, the rout was on.

The 1959 season started the ball rolling, and Haines's team grew to be recognized as a perennial power. In 1961, the team achieved its first undefeated season at 8-0-2. It was Dover's first undefeated squad since 1942. In all, Haines would lead Dover to two undefeated seasons and three other years in which the team went 9-1. In five of Haines's twelve seasons as head coach, the team went 9-1 or better, including a 7-4-1 mark against the Quakers.

Included in Haines's outstanding career at Dover were two fantastic Dover-Phila games in 1965 and 1967. The 1965 game was first a nightmare and then a dream come true for the Tornadoes. After fumbling on the goal line with less than a minute to play, crushing their hopes, New Phila returned the favor, and the Tornadoes won in dramatic fashion. The 1967 game was a 6–0 squeaker won on a second quarter touchdown by halfback Colby Byrom. Byrom's run secured Haines's best season at Dover with a 10-0 record.

Despite all his success, there comes a time for change in everyone's life. In 1970, the Haines family left Dover to move closer to his wife's family in California. Dick Haines accepted the job of head football coach at Vista High School, thirty-five miles north of San Diego. Much like at Dover, it didn't take long for Coach Haines's winning ways to take hold. Vista High

An Era of Change

won the State Championship under Coach Haines in 1974 and 1985. Haines remained its coach until his retirement in 1995. During his years as a high school football coach, Haines's overall record of 320-126-12 makes him one of the winningest high school football coaches of all time.

1963: New Phila, 12; Dover, 8

The 1963 victory of the New Philadelphia Quakers was as unexpected as a snowstorm in mid-July. Throughout the history of the rivalry, very few games can be classified as true upsets; 1963 is definitely one of those games.

Coming into the final game of the 1963 season, the New Phila Quakers had struggled mightily. They were decimated by injuries and had managed only one win to go with six losses and two ties. Led by coach Al Christopher in his third year, the team had never managed a winning season for its coach. In addition, Coach Christopher was yet to taste victory against his crosstown rival. Even worse for the Red and Black was a dismal streak of twenty consecutive losses at all levels to the boys from Dover over the previous five years. The streak meant that no New Phila team at any level, high school

The 1963 New Philadelphia High School football team. *Courtesy of the Quaker Foundation.*

or middle school, had defeated a Dover grid team since the current seniors were themselves middle schoolers.

On top of the streak, New Phila had to deal with the loss of one of its best players. Terry Keiser was a 155-pound senior halfback for the Quakers and one of the team's few bright spots in 1963. He led the team in scoring and yards rushing and was among the Quaker leaders in tackles. He was also ineligible for the 1963 game. Keiser's ineligibility stemmed from a poor decision he made after the 1962 game. In November 1962, Keiser got into a fight with a Dover boy. When he was called in front of Judge Ralph Finley, Keiser received a rather unorthodox punishment. As part of his probation, Keiser was barred from playing in the 1963 Dover-Phila game. Despite numerous requests from members of the community, Finley refused to give in. New Phila would be without one of its key players. All of these factors combined to make a Quaker victory so improbable.

For its part, Dover was strong and steady in 1963. It was led by coach Dick Haines in his sixth season with the Tornadoes. The team carried a record of 7-1-1 and was in second place in the Cardinal Conference. Its only loss of the year came at the hands of eventual conference champion Ashland in week eight. Offensively, Dover was led by sophomore quarterback Steve Trustdorf and seniors Terry Simmons and Don Ammiller. Although it was not playing for a championship, a win over the Quakers would complete a fine season at 8-1-1.

In what was a surprise to almost everyone, the game was dominated by the underdog Quakers. Dover would reach New Phila territory only once, and Dover's young quarterback, Steve Trustdorf, would fail to complete a single pass, throwing two interceptions. Both of New Phila's touchdown drives were set up by turnovers.

The game didn't see much action in the first period until the closing seconds, when New Phila's Joe Moestra intercepted a pass at Dover's forty-eight. As time expired in the quarter, Moestra returned the pick to Dover's thirty-five, setting up the first Quaker touchdown. Taking over with good field position, the Quakers featured an eight-man line. The addition of the extra man up front was an adjustment that the Quakers had not used prior to the big game. Utilizing this run first formation, the Quakers would propel two of their running backs over one hundred yards and dominate the line of scrimmage. This was the case on the nine-play punishing drive capped by a

An Era of Change

Dave Moreland four-yard touchdown, giving the Red and Black a 6–0 lead. A failed conversion attempt kept the score 6–0.

The Quakers would score again quickly, as they again capitalized on a Dover mistake. On the very next possession by the Tornadoes, the ball slipped out of Trustdorf's hands and was recovered by New Phila's Larry Denmon. Again, the bruising running attack went to work, this time from the Dover thirty-nine. It took the Quakers only five plays to score, with the touchdown coming on a two-yard plunge by Dale "Poochie" Tate. The big play of the drive was a thirty-two-yard run by Moreland. Again, the extra point failed, and the Quakers led 12–0.

The score remained 12–0 into the third quarter when Dover came alive. On only the second play after the half, Moreland fumbled, and Dover's Duke Strickmaker recovered at the Quaker thirty. Six plays later, Strickmaker again took the ball, this time going in for a one-yard touchdown to cut the lead to 12–6. A tackle-eligible pass to Mike Contini gave the Tornadoes another two points, and Phila's lead was cut to 12–8.

After the quick start, both teams' offenses bogged down, and neither threatened to score until the very end of the quarter. At the close of the third period, Phila's Moestra picked off another Trustdorf pass, and it appeared as if the outcome would be the same as his first interception. New Phila took over at the forty-five and drove all the way to Dover's one-yard line. Disaster struck on the goal line for the Quakers, though, as the ball slipped out of Moreland's hands and was recovered by the Tornadoes' Terry Simmons.

Despite its luck on the one-yard line, Dover was never really able to gain momentum offensively, and it remained unable to move the ball. Late in the fourth, New Phila sophomore Tim Halter sealed the game when he recovered a Dover fumble on the Tornado sixteen-yard line. With less than a minute remaining, New Phila ran out the clock and won 12–8.

The Quakers were led in their upset win by a collection of unlikely heroes. Joe Moestra's two interceptions were keys to the New Phila win. Moestra, the son of a song-writing preacher, was playing in his first game since mid-September, when he suffered an ankle injury. On offense, the Quakers were led by the running of Dave Moreland and Dale "Poochie" Tate. Moreland carried the ball twenty-seven times for 122 yards, while Tate racked up good yardage, gaining 102 on twenty-eight carries. The effort of Moreland must have come as a real surprise to the Tornadoes. Prior to the Dover-Phila game, the 185-pound sophomore had played on offense in only one other game that season, an embarrassing 28–6 loss to Uhrichsville in week nine. Moreland wasn't even listed as a starter in the days prior to the game.

Led by a relatively unknown cast of characters, the 1963 Quakers pulled off one of the greatest upsets in the history of the rivalry.

1965: Dover, 14; New Phila, 12

The 1965 game should have been an upset. There is no conceivable reason the New Phila Quakers should not have beaten the favored Tornadoes. So what saved the Tornadoes that rainy November night? What saved them was quite possibly the most bizarre ending in the 110-year history of the rivalry.

Coming into their 1965 matchup, the Dover Tornadoes were loaded on offense. They had scored 312 points in only nine games, putting up gaudy rushing numbers. Paul Huff, Dover's 215-pound fullback, would finish the season with nearly 1,100 yards. In addition to Huff, Dover was blessed with backs like Dick Horn, Jim Morrow, John Reese and the speedy Jeff Souers. At quarterback for the Tornadoes was three-year starter and senior Steve Trustdorf. Even with such a talented running game, Trustdorf still managed to pass for 854 yards and seven touchdowns.

New Philadelphia had been less impressive in 1965. Led by co-captains Jerry Bower and Tim Halter, the Quakers had a 6-3 record coming into the big game. New Phila was coached by Al Christopher in his fifth season as the Quaker mentor. Against Dover, he was 1-2-1, with his only win coming in 1963 in one of the biggest upsets in the history of the rivalry. With a tie in 1964 and with talented quarterback Nick Incarnato behind center, Christopher looked to pull another upset.

Over seven thousand fans came out to support their teams at a wet and rainy Crater Stadium. To the shock of the hometown fans, the Quakers looked to have the upper hand in each of the first three quarters. Only a wild finish by the Tornadoes gave the hometown fans reason to cheer.

Dover's first score saw the offense doing exactly what the hometown fans had come to expect. The Tornadoes took the ball on their own thirteen and moved it all the way to the Quaker five. Leading the charge was Dover's stable of thoroughbred runners. With Huff, Horn and Reese moving the

An Era of Change

ball, Dover looked unstoppable. That is, until it reached the five and Phila tightened up.

On fourth and five, Dover trotted out kicker and exchange student Niels Nielsen to attempt the field goal and give the Crimson Tornadoes a 3–0 lead. To everyone's surprise, backup quarterback Ken Korns, in the role of holder, took the snap and rolled out to pass. Korns found Lloyd "Bud" Beaber in the end zone and fired a strike for a six-yard touchdown. Just like that, the Tornadoes led 6–0. A fumbled pitch on the conversion attempt kept the score at 6–0. No one would have guessed that the Tornadoes wouldn't score again until the closing moments of the game.

New Phila didn't waste any time answering the Tornado touchdown on its very next drive. The Quakers received the kickoff and drove all the way from their own twenty-two to tie the game. The tying score came on a Nick Incarnato pass to Joe Richards for a twenty-yard touchdown. Unfortunately, Incarnato's kicking wasn't as accurate as his passing, and the extra point attempt sailed wide left. With only 2:35 left in the half, neither team would score again, as they went into the break with the score tied at 6–6.

As the second half began, New Philadelphia came out strong behind the running of Joe Richards. The Quakers marched the ball all the way down the field to Dover's twenty. On the twenty-yard line, Coach Christopher took a gamble on a halfback pass that paid big dividends. Jamie McGarry hit sophomore Jay Force with a twenty-yard strike that put the Red and Black ahead 12–6.

After an exchange of punts, Dover put together a good drive behind the running of Huff and junior Jeff Souers. Starting on their own thirty, Huff and Souers carried the Tornadoes all the way to their opponent's nine-yard line before the visitor's defense again stepped up. This time, it was a big fourth and four hold that gave the Quakers the ball on downs.

Taking over inside the ten, the Quakers were unable to gain a first down and were forced into a fourth down situation on their own thirteen. Electing to punt, New Phila made the first of two errors that would eventually cost it the game. Playing for field position, Coach Christopher instructed his kicker to take the snap and take a knee in the end zone. The play gave Dover two points and bought New Phila several precious yards to hopefully drive the Tornadoes back into their own territory. In theory, Coach Christopher's call is not that unorthodox. In a close game that has been dominated by the defense, it's not a terrible decision to try and pin your opponent deep and avoid the potential of a blocked kick.

Regardless of his reasoning or intent, the benefit of field position was negated when Dover's Jim Morrow executed a big return on the ensuing kickoff. With the score at 12–8, the safety allowed New Phila to kick off to the Tornadoes from its own twenty. Morrow received the ball at the Dover thirty-yard line, eluded several Quaker defenders and broke off a forty-yard return. As Dover's offense strolled onto the field, it had first and ten on the Quaker thirty.

Sparked by Morrow's return, the Tornadoes needed only seven plays to take the ball all the way to their opponent's one-yard line. From the one, just as Dover looked to take the lead, disaster struck. Trustdorf fumbled the snap, and Phila recovered with less than a minute remaining. All the Quakers had to do was hold on for one minute and pull off the upset.

With victory all but secured, the Quakers threw it all away as they fumbled the ball back to the Tornadoes with twenty seconds left on the clock. Dover's Ron Dessecker recovered, and Paul Huff scored from a yard out on the final play of the game. The combination of the backfired safety call and the crucial fumble managed to snatch defeat from the jaws of victory. The Tornadoes won the game 14–12 in the most unexpected finish in the history of the great rivalry.

1966: The Dual Band Show

With all of the focus going toward the Dover and New Phila football players, it is sometimes easy to forget another important element of the rivalry. While the players fight it out on the gridiron, the two school's bands hold their annual competition at halftime. The halftime show, featuring performances by both bands, has long been a traditional part of the rivalry. If not an outright competition, the bands' performances do provide one school a sort of bragging right until the two bands face off again the following year.

This tradition of dueling bands was commonplace at halftime until 1966. That year, in an act of absolute sacrilege to some alumni and former band members, the two marching bands combined to perform a dual halftime show. While it wasn't new for both bands to perform together, which they

An Era of Change

The Dover and New Philadelphia marching bands perform together at halftime of the 1966 Dover-Phila Game. *Courtesy of Fred and Caroline Delphia.*

had done prior to the game on numerous occasions, the idea of the annual halftime show being a joint effort was unheard-of.

Organized by two young band directors, Fred Delphia of Dover and Robert Bianco of New Phila, the idea came from a band show at Massillon that featured a combined performance by the Canton South High School and Louisville High Schools bands. At the time of the proposed Dover-Phila combined show, both Delphia and Bianco were in their first years at their respective schools and had no idea that anyone would object to a combined show. Object they did. Both directors and their schools were inundated with letters and requests to scrap the idea. The two local newspapers also received many letters claiming that the dual show was "ruining the tradition." Some even went as far as to sarcastically call for the two schools to just combine and forget the whole rivalry. In one letter, a Dover alumnus and former band member compared the joint show to asking the Ohio State and Michigan bands to play together.

When game night finally arrived, both directors decided to go ahead with their planned dual show, even with the outrage in the newspapers. Although there had been some jostling back and forth between the two bands during practices prior to the performance, when it came game night, both sides were all business. The 160-member combined band performed songs such as "Days of Glory," "Fly Me to the Moon" and "Spanish Flea." Their finale was a rousing rendition of "America the Beautiful," complete with majorettes wielding flaming torches and aerial bombs and fireworks.

As the show ended, both directors held their breath, not knowing what to expect from the crowd. What they received for their efforts was a standing ovation from both sides. In addition to the response from the fans, both bands also received many positive reviews from the local newspapers. They called the dual show "tremendous" and the "show of shows." Despite the positive response from the fans on game night, Delphia remembers meeting Bianco at the conclusion of the show to shake hands. As the bands headed back to their respective sides, both men commented, "Never again." Their promise has held, as the two bands have been back to their traditional halftime performances ever since.

1967: Dover, 6; New Phila, 0

In his column the week leading up to the game, legendary local sportswriter Ed Degraw shared the following: "It will be too late for excuses Saturday." No truer words have been spoken in the history of the rivalry. This was an especially potent statement in 1967. Coming into the big game, Dover was the heavy favorite, but a determined New Philadelphia squad nearly upset the Tornadoes by leaving it all out on the field. In this classic, neither team needed to make any excuses.

The year 1967 was another great one for Dick Haines and the Dover Tornadoes. Dover was 9-0 coming into the game. It was ranked fifth in the state and looked to gain another Cardinal Conference Championship. On the field, the Tornadoes were led by one of the most talented offenses in the school's history. It featured junior quarterback Rich Trustdorf, who finished

An Era of Change

The 1967 Dover High School football team. *Courtesy of Denny Rubright.*

the season with 832 yards and eleven touchdowns. More importantly, the team was loaded with running backs. Leading the charge for Dover was all-Ohio running back Dave Keitch, who rushed for over 1,000 yards and seventeen touchdowns in 1967. Not far behind Keitch was the speedy Colby Byrom, who chipped in with an additional 692 yards rushing. Opening holes for the two talented backs was fullback and co-captain Bill Hawk. Behind its strong running game, the 1967 Tornado offense would finish close to Haines's 1965 team by scoring 314 points.

On defense, the Tornadoes were loaded as well. They featured Hawk, Darrell Davis and all-Ohio end Rich Cappel. When speaking of Cappel, Coach Haines referred to him as "my all-state head hunter." Led by such a talented group, Dover gave up only forty-four points all season and proceeded to shut out four of its ten opponents. The most points scored on the Tornadoes all year was eight.

With all of Dover's impressive statistics and its undefeated and untied record, it should come as no surprise that New Philadelphia was a big underdog in the contest. The Quakers had won only two games coming in and lost the week before the Dover-Phila game to Claymont, 7–0. Dover, on the other hand, had clobbered the Mustangs 56–0. One of New Phila's biggest challenges in 1967 was change. The team that took the field that year featured almost an entirely new backfield and many new linemen. Graduation had not been kind to the Quakers. Of those who remained,

The Dover-Phila Football Rivalry

New Phila relied on a young cast of characters like sophomore quarterback Joe Streb, junior fullback Mark Moreland and quarterback turned half back Greg Brown. On defense, the Quakers were led by linebacker John Frenzel.

The New Philadelphia Quakers also welcomed a new coach in 1967. Sam Miller took over on July 10, after the abrupt departure of coach Al Christopher. Miller's promotion to head coach was a whirlwind affair. He received the nod only four days after Coach Christopher announced he was leaving the Red and Black to become an assistant at Kent State University. Not in the position to conduct a coaching search in mid-July, Miller, who was an assistant under Christopher, got the promotion. In addition to his work under Christopher, Miller was a New Phila alumnus who played under coach Bill Kidd. Along with his connection to Kidd, Miller was also teammates with two other New Phila legends, Bill "Cannonball" Cooper and Ward Holdsworth. Despite his connections and great pedigree, Miller struggled in his first year at the helm, but perhaps because of his history, he recognized one important fact: a win over Dover and no one would remember the Quakers' struggles.

A rabid crowd of nearly seven thousand fans showed up at Crater Stadium to watch their Crimson Tornados try to complete their first undefeated and untied season since 1942. Eventually, they would get what they came for, but only after a surprising—and some would say inspired—performance by the Quaker defense.

If one were judging the game by Dover's first drive, then one would never believe that the final score would be 6–0. Taking the ball at their own thirty-three, the Tornadoes put together a sixteen-play drive that took them all the way to the Quaker thirteen. Within striking distance, though, the Phila defense tightened up, and Dover stalled. This would become a recurring theme that night.

There wasn't much else by way of offense the rest of the first period, as New Phila's defense held tight and its offense couldn't hold onto the ball. The Quakers fumbled twice in the first quarter. That all changed quickly at the beginning of the second period.

After a Bill Hawk rumble for a first down at the New Phila forty-six, Colby Byrom made the play of the game. On first down, Dover handed the ball to the speedy Byrom, who managed to outrun the entire New Philadelphia defense. Forty-six yards later, Dover led 6–0 and looked to have found its

An Era of Change

rhythm. After the extra point failed, the score remained 6–0. Who would have guessed that Byrom's big run would be the difference in the game?

After receiving the kickoff from the Tornadoes, the Quakers proved that they wouldn't be intimidated by Dover's big score. They put together a drive of their own that went all the way to the Tornado eleven-yard line. Although they eventually turned the ball over on downs, the drive ate up a good chunk of the second period and took away Dover's momentum. The teams would exchange punts to close out the quarter, and at the half the score remained 6–0 in favor of the Tornadoes.

In the third period, both teams moved the ball effectively, yet neither was able to put any points on the board. Both defenses had an uncanny ability to make big plays and tighten up right as their opponent seemed to be getting somewhere. One of those big plays, and a crushing blow to the Quakers, was made by Dover's Dave Keitch. With New Phila within sight of the goal line, Keitch intercepted a pass at Dover's own seven, ending the Quaker threat. With only 1:19 left in the third, it was a very costly turnover.

Taking over at its own seven, Dover executed a clock-eating drive to start the fourth. Again, though, the Quakers tightened up in their own territory, and Dover was forced to punt from the Quaker thirty-six. A great punt pinned the Quakers deep in their own territory at the four-yard line. Despite struggling on offense again, New Phila was able to keep its drive alive with a little chicanery.

Looking like they would punt, New Phila's Greg Brown took the snap and instead rolled out to pass. He found end Terry Heverly, who pulled in the pass and picked up a Quaker first down at their own thirty-four. The hopes of the Red and Black were still alive. Even with the gained momentum of the big first down, the offense was still unable to move the ball, and New Phila was eventually forced to punt, ending its drive at the forty-five.

After Dover's powerful offense was stuffed again, New Phila received the punt and would get one final opportunity. The Quakers took advantage of their last chance, driving deep into Dover territory. The big play of the drive was a Terry Heverly catch that gave the Quakers a first and ten with only seventeen seconds left on the clock. On the very next play, Greg Brown dropped back to pass looking for an open receiver. He saw no one so he made the smart decision to unload the ball out of bounds. Unfortunately, he didn't put enough air under the ball, and it bounced off one of his teammates' helmets. Dover's Darrell Davis came down with deflection, securing the win and the perfect season for the Tornadoes.

THE DOVER-PHILA FOOTBALL RIVALRY

1969: NEW PHILA, 8; DOVER, 0

The 1969 matchup between Dover's Tornadoes and New Philadelphia's Quakers is perhaps one of the most anticipated games in the entire history of the storied rivalry. It featured both individual and team storylines, great record-setting players and major implications in regards to the Cardinal Conference. For the first time since both teams had been playing together in the conference, the championship would be settled on the field in the final week of the season. This one was about more than just bragging rights.

Coming into the game, Dover looked to continue its dominance under head coach Dick Haines. Although no one knew it at the time, Haines would be coaching in his last game as the Dover mentor. Following the season, his family relocated to California. Despite what was surely a disappointing finale in Dover, Haines left the school as its all-time leader in wins with an overall record of 90-25-6.

As the teams prepared for the big game in 1969, thoughts weren't on Haines; they were on Dover's stellar defense. That year, the Tornadoes allowed only eighteen points coming into the game with New Phila and had shut out seven of its first nine opponents. Only Cincinnati Withrow managed to score in double digits against the Tornadoes, and the defense had not given up a point since week two.

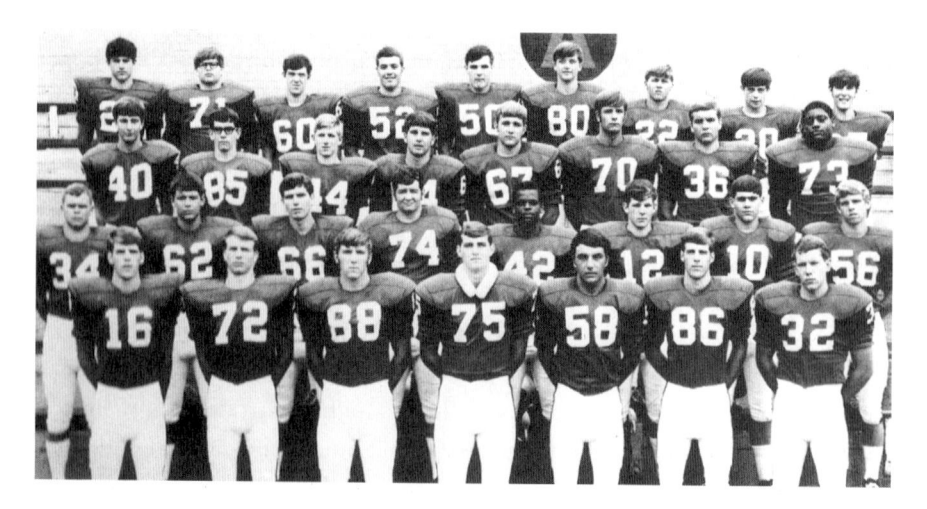

The 1969 New Philadelphia High School football team. *Courtesy of the Quaker Foundation.*

An Era of Change

On offense, Dover was led by junior quarterback Al Trustdorf for most of the season. Tragedy struck, though, when Trustdorf broke his wrist in week eight against Ashland. The Dover quarterback was a leader on the field and the fourth of four brothers to play for the Tornadoes. His replacement was Dan Tarulli. Even without Trustdorf, Dover ran all over Canton Timken in the week before the Phila game, with a final score of 32–0. Also on offense, Dover featured leading ground gainer Randy Swinderman and talented end Steve Mastin. Mastin was one of the stars in the 1968 game when he pulled in a pass from Trustdorf's brother Rich and scampered sixty-eight yards for a touchdown.

While Dover was recognized for its stingy defense, New Philadelphia featured a multitalented offense for coach Sam Miller. Miller was in his third year as the Quaker coach and was still looking for his first win against the Tornadoes. Despite his struggles against Dover, Miller had made a definite difference in the Quaker program. After his first team went just 2-8, Miller motivated his Quakers to a 7-3 record in 1968 and an excellent mark of 8-1 coming into the 1969 season finale. More important than his overall record, Miller's team was undefeated in the Cardinal Conference and looking to earn its first conference championship since it joined the league in 1963.

The leader of the Quakers' powerful offense was quarterback Joe Streb. Streb was in his third year as the Quaker starter and in his last chance to defeat the Tornadoes. Joining Streb in the backfield was fullback Dave Korns and tailback Bill Seabrook. Seabrook was outstanding during the 1969 season. With one game to play, he needed only seventy yards to pass Bill "Cannonball" Cooper's single season rushing record of 1,215 yards.

While all the hype was about the New Phila offense and the Dover defense, it would end up being the underrated New Phila defense that would win the game for the Quakers. From the opening kickoff, it became clear that the game would not feature a lot of scoring.

After exchanging punts and a failure to move the ball on the part of both teams, the game's first big break came with less than two minutes remaining in the first quarter. On the play, New Philadelphia attempted a pitchout from its own six-yard line that was fumbled and recovered by the Tornadoes. Dover took over with first and goal.

Dover pushed the ball forward from the six during the next two plays before disaster struck on third down. With third and goal from the New

The Dover-Phila Football Rivalry

Phila two-yard line, the Tornadoes put the ball on the turf. Jerry Platz recovered for the Quakers, ending Dover's hopes for the game's first scoring opportunity. Both teams' fumbles would be the first of many that evening. The Dover and New Phila offenses ended the game with four fumbles each.

Beginning their drive from their own two-yard line, New Philadelphia was looking for some wiggle room. That's exactly what it got when fullback Dave Korns broke loose to the Quaker forty-five. Although the drive didn't end in any points for the Quakers, it did allow them a leg up in the all-important field position battle.

After Dover was unable to move the ball, New Phila would get the ball back toward the end of the half. They drove all the way down to Dover's eleven before the defense tightened, stopping the Quakers on fourth down. Taking over on downs, Dover was able to move the ball out to the Quaker forty-five before time expired in the half. Little did Dover know that this drive would be the closest it would get to the Quaker goal line for the remainder of the game. At the half, the two teams remained deadlocked at 0–0.

After the half, the Tornadoes kicked off to a fired-up New Phila squad. The Quakers took the kickoff at their own twenty-five-yard line and put together one of the best drives of the game. They proceeded to move the ball all the way to Dover's one-yard line in a masterful fourteen-play drive. Once they reached the one, though, a penalty pushed the Quakers back to the fifteen, forcing a passing situation. Streb completed the pass, but the receiver coughed up the ball. Dover recovered, ending the New Phila threat.

As the clocked ticked away in the third quarter, with the score still tied 0–0, Dover looked to regain momentum when it pinned the Quakers deep. The poor field position was the result of a booming kick by Dover's Steve Mastin. Mastin uncorked a fifty-eight-yard punt that pinned the Quakers all the way back at their eighteen.

As the fourth quarter began, both teams continued to struggle on offense, exchanging punts. Action picked up again, though, with five minutes left when Dover seemed to catch a break. The Tornadoes intercepted a Quaker pass and sent the offense on the field. Unfortunately for the Tornadoes, their own turnover woes would continue. The offense again lost possession on a fumble. This time, they gave the Quakers an excellent opportunity with just thirty-one yards separating them from the game-winning score.

An Era of Change

It looked as though another quick reversal of fortune would happen as Streb fumbled on Phila's first play from scrimmage. This time, though, luck was on the side of the Quakers. Streb's fumble bounced harmlessly out of bounds, leaving the Quakers with second and two at Dover's twenty-five. From there, Streb and Korns took over, pounding the Tornado defense. With only 1:46 remaining in the game, Streb plunged in for the game's first score from two yards out. On the conversion try, Streb connected with Danny Evans and the Quaker lead grew to 8–0.

With less than two minutes to play, Dover received the kickoff and got to work. It moved the ball downfield quickly on a hook-and-ladder play. Tarulli hit Cliff Easlick with a pass, and Easlick lateraled to Reggie Hunter for a nice gain. Putting the ball in the air again on the next play, Dover's fate was sealed. New Phila intercepted a Tarulli pass, ending the Tornadoes' hopes. Streb ran out the remaining 1:45, and the Quakers were Cardinal Conference Champions.

For his efforts, Streb was named the game's Most Valuable Player. In the game, he rushed for 118 yards and the game's only touchdown. The quarterback also completed four of five passes for twenty-seven yards. For his part, Bill Seabrook just missed Cooper's rushing record. He finished nineteen yards shy of the mark. Throughout the contest, Seabrook was Dover's number one target, clearing the way for the outstanding games of Streb and Korns, who added eighty-three yards in the win. On defense, Benny Cox intercepted two passes for the Quakers.

4
THE CARDINAL CONFERENCE YEARS
1970–1989

1972: NEW PHILA, 15; DOVER, 14

When it comes to great games, 1972 has everything you could ever ask for. That year, we saw a great comeback, a spectacular and unexpected big play and a game-winning score inside of two minutes. As a true fan of the game, it's tough to find a contest that has more to offer. The 1972 Dover-Phila game surely ranks as a classic in the rivalry.

The sixty-eighth clash between the crosstown rivals was played on November 10 on a cold, wet and muddy field at Quaker stadium. Beginning about two hours before kickoff, the rain commenced, producing a steady downpour that drenched fans and players alike. Despite the rains, over eight thousand spectators braved the elements to see the 5-4 Tornadoes play the 4-5 Quakers. Although both teams had struggled throughout the season, both locker rooms knew that a victory over their archrivals would make the season a success.

New Phila came into the big rivalry game under head coach Gary "Sam" Miller. A 1953 graduate of New Phila, Miller was in his last year coaching the school. His career record of 36-23-1 made him the third-winningest coach in the school's history when he left after the 1972 season. He was also looking to tie a mark that only coach Bill Kidd had managed. A victory over Dover would give the Phils five consecutive years without a losing season.

Coming into the game, New Phila looked to senior quarterback Greg Turner and fellow senior Jeff Tucker. The Quakers would also rely on the

THE DOVER-PHILA FOOTBALL RIVALRY

The 1972 New Philadelphia High School football team. *Courtesy of the Quaker Foundation.*

tough running of sophomore Jeff Dummermuth. Dummermuth had only broken into the starting lineup two weeks earlier as the result of injuries. Prior to week seven, New Phila had relied on the running of Greg Chek and Dave Doughten, but after both were injured, Dummermuth got his shot. He would make the most of it in the Dover-Phila game.

On the opposite sideline, Dover was led by the fantastic duo of senior quarterback Dave Migliore and sophomore running back Dean Richards. Both men would go on to Division I college programs, with Migliore playing at the University of Pittsburgh and Richards at the University of Maryland. The head coach of the Tornadoes was Tom Redman. In his third year at the school, Redman had a record of 18-11, with two wins in a row over the Quakers.

When kickoff finally came that rainy night, Dover's Tornadoes got off to a fast start in the first half. With a little over two minutes to play in the first quarter, Dave Migliore broke free for the game's first touchdown. The touchdown went for twenty-three yards, giving the Tornadoes an early lead.

Dover's second score was both set up and executed by the outstanding Richards. On the final play of the first quarter, Richards picked off a pass from New Phila's Greg Turner on his team's own twenty-two-yard line. The Tornadoes then began a seventy-eight-yard march that was capped off by a Richards's touchdown. The score came on a four-yard option pitch from Migliore and gave Dover a commanding 14–0 lead with less than three minutes remaining in the half.

Once again, New Philadelphia could do nothing with the ball, and Dover went into the locker room maintaining its 14–0 lead in dominating

The Cardinal Conference Years

fashion. The Tornadoes held a huge differential in time of possession and allowed Phila only two first downs the entire first half. In addition, Richards had been a workhorse, toting the ball seventeen times for ninety yards. It must've looked to the Phila faithful like it would take a miracle to wrestle the game from Dover.

New Phila's big break and the major shift in momentum that night came on a Dover punt with a little over nine minutes left in the third. Dover's punter, Jeff Korns, dropped back to punt from his team's forty-yard line, but the ball traveled only seventeen yards before hitting the ground. It was the type of play that fans of the game are used to seeing several times each game. The ball bounces aimlessly around for a couple of yards before the kicking team downs it and possession changes hands. This time, though, New Phila free safety Jeff Tucker decided to take matters into his own hands.

It was one of those plays that make a player a hero in a rivalry game, but it is also one of those plays where the same player could have just as easily cost his team the game and given the Tornadoes a three-touchdown lead. As it happened, Tucker picked up the bouncing ball and raced toward the right sidelines. Before the Tornadoes knew what had happened, Tucker had picked up a couple of blockers and was racing down the field. He was able to outrun any other Dover defenders, scoring from seventy yards out and putting the Quakers on the board. A successful two-point conversion run on the next play drew New Philadelphia even closer as the score now read 14–8.

What would be the game-wining score for the Quakers came late in the fourth quarter. A Dover player bobbled the ball deep in his own territory, and New Phila's Dan Rufenacht recovered on the Tornado twenty-four-yard line. After a sequence of short gains by halfback Tucker and tailback Dummermuth, New Phila faced a crucial fourth down and three with only three minutes remaining in the game. The Quakers were able to answer this challenge behind the running of senior quarterback Greg Turner. Turner converted the fourth down try and gave his team a first and goal from the five.

With only 1:49 to play in the game, New Phila's sophomore running back, Dummermuth, scored over left tackle to tie the game at 14–14. It wouldn't stay tied long, though, as kicker Tim McCoy trotted onto the field, in his perfectly clean white uniform, and converted the extra point, giving the Quakers a one-point lead with very little time remaining.

Dover did have one last chance that evening. Migliore led his team to the Dover forty-nine-yard line, but on the ensuing play, Migliore was sacked all the way back at the thirty-eight. Facing fourth and long, Migliore dropped back and attempted to hit wingback Greg Gurney downfield. The ball fell to the turf, and the Tornadoes' last-ditch effort was over. While Phila fans were jubilant, the Dover bench was irate, calling for pass interference. The call never came, and New Phila took over and ran out the game clock.

The 1972 game is a true classic and a great example of how stats don't always tell the story. That evening, the Tornadoes outgained the Quakers 218 yards to 64 on offense. In addition, despite the loss, the game's MVP was Dover's Dean Richards. Richards accounted for 99 yards rushing on twenty-two carries. He would've cracked the century mark, but leg cramps in the third quarter kept him out of much of the remainder of the game.

1974: NEW PHILA, 7; DOVER, 0

The year 1974 was the quintessential defensive battle between two very good teams. It was also a very controversial game. Even if both teams weren't undefeated when they met in early November, a muddy field and a contested touchdown would still make this one a classic.

The 1970s were great years in the Cardinal Conference for both the Dover Tornadoes and the New Phila Quakers. Between 1974 and 1979, the conference champion was decided by the annual crosstown rivalry game in

The 1974 New Philadelphia High School football team. *Courtesy of Denny Rubright.*

The Cardinal Conference Years

The 1974 Dover High School football team. *Courtesy of Denny Rubright.*

five of six seasons. The conference was formed in 1959 with four charter members, including Dover. New Philadelphia joined in December 1961, bringing the total number of teams to seven. Dover and New Phila both remained part of the Cardinal Conference until its demise after the 1986–87 school year. Over the course of its affiliation, Dover won ten Cardinal Conference championships, while New Philadelphia won five.

The 1974 rivalry game marked the second time that Dover and New Phila would square off for the conference championship. The first time was in 1969, when the Quakers pulled out a tight 8–0 win. It is also the only time in the history of the rivalry that both teams were undefeated and ranked in the top ten in the Associated Press state football poll.

Coming into the 1974 game, the Quakers had a stellar record of 8-0-1. This accomplishment was on the heels of a 4-6 season in 1973. Coach John Behling had worked his players hard, and they had responded with an outstanding turnaround. The Quakers were led by quarterback Les Freshwater, tight end Ted Metcalf and fullback Phil Tidrick. Tidrick also handled the kicking duties for the Quakers.

Dover was again led by head coach Tom Redman. Redman had guided the Tornadoes to a 9-1 record in 1973, including a 17–0 victory over the county-seaters. On offense, the Tornadoes featured quarterback Mike Perkowski and fullback Gene Reese, but Dover's real star was tailback Dean Richards. Richards was in his third and final year as a starter. The senior would score twenty-eight touchdowns and rush for 2,646 yards during his prep career.

The Dover-Phila Football Rivalry

It's not uncommon for touchdowns to be scored early in defensive battles. Usually when two teams are allowed to settle in, especially two teams with good defenses, they give up very few points. The 1974 Dover-Phila game is an excellent representation of this theory. The only score of the game came on the very first drive. After that, the game was entirely dominated by the two defenses.

On the very first possession of the game, the New Philadelphia Quakers received the kickoff and drove sixty-nine yards in sixteen plays for the only score that evening. The drive, though, was not without drama. It began on New Phila's own thirty-one after Dover's kickoff. New Phila plugged away, driving all the way down to Dover's thirty-seven-yard line before its progress screeched to a halt.

After being held on third down, New Phila lined up in its punt formation with Tidrick back deep to kick. With a fourth and five situation, Dover's coaches and players assumed the Quakers would play it safe and try to pin it deep. Dover had another thing coming.

In an incredibly gutsy move, New Phila's coach called a fake punt pass with a full eight minutes remaining in the first quarter. On the play, Phil Tidrick took the snap and, instead of punting, looked to pass. As he dropped back, he located receiver Jim Bird, who was looping out to the left side. Tidrick set and fired a wounded duck to Bird, who ran to the Dover twenty-six for a first down. Although his pass may not have been pretty, it was effective, and New Philadelphia's drive remained alive.

After grinding out the remaining yardage to the two, Jerry Brown cartwheeled into the end zone for the game's only score. There was only one problem with the play: the head linesman signaled that Brown had lost possession of the ball before scoring. For a few brief seconds, it looked like Dover would catch a break. Unfortunately for the Tornadoes, the linesman was overruled, and it was determined that the ground had caused the fumble. The touchdown, and the Quaker lead, would stand. Tidrick put the extra point through the uprights, and Phila held a 7–0 lead on the unbeaten Tornadoes.

The rest of the game included very few highlights for either team. Dover had little success on offense, gaining only 163 yards in the game. Even Dean Richards was held in check as he gained only forty-six yards on thirteen carries. The closest Dover came to scoring that night was a fourth and two at the Quaker fourteen. New Phila's defense tightened up, and Dover turned the ball over on downs.

While the Quaker defense would get the credit for the win, the Dover defense also came up big following that first drive. They gave up only 203 yards of offense, and Tornado defender Jeff Mills twice intercepted the Quakers. The second interception came on Dover's eight-yard line and ended a potential scoring threat.

Ironically, the MVP of the game was New Philadelphia's leading receiver of the season. It's ironic in that Ted Metcalf didn't catch a single pass in the game. Coming into the big game, Metcalf led the team with twenty-six catches for 539 yards, but in the Dover-Phila game, it was Metcalf's defensive skills that were on display. He came up with six big tackles from his defensive end spot, earning the game's MVP award.

While there weren't many fireworks during the game, the same couldn't be said afterward. When talking to the press, Dover coach Tom Redman was livid. Coach Redman refused to concede victory to the Red and Black, arguing against the first touchdown on the grounds that Brown had fumbled before he scored. Although he did credit the New Phila team and coaches, the touchdown call was just something Redman couldn't accept. He stated, "I won't concede the victory and neither will the kids. I'd rather the game not have been decided on something controversial. If they had gone down and got another one, okay, but they didn't."

In addition to the controversial call, Redman also brought up another rumor that had swirled through the community in the week leading up to the game. There were whispers in Dover prior to kickoff that New Phila had watered down the field in an effort to slow Dover's high-powered offense. Although the field was muddy, New Phila denied doing any such thing. For his two cents, Redman weighed in. He acknowledged that he had heard the rumor and stated, "If I find out it's true and we lack speed next year, they will be playing in mud up to their knees." Although the coach later reversed his comments, the damage was done. Fans to this day still debate the controversial touchdown and the allegations of doctoring the field.

Lost in all the controversy surrounding the 1974 game is the significance of its outcome to the New Philadelphia Quakers. The game gave them the outright Cardinal Conference Championship and a shot at the state playoffs.

The playoff opportunity hinged on the following day's Massillon-McKinley game. A win by 9-0 McKinley and New Phila was out, but a Massillon win put it in. In a game that New Phila's coach John Behling saw in person, the upstart 5-4 Massillon squad upset the top-ranked Bulldogs, sending the Quakers to the playoffs. Although they were defeated the following week by Upper Arlington, qualifying for the state playoffs was an important milestone for the Phila program.

1978: New Phila, 13; Dover, 10

The 1978 Dover-Phila contest provided yet another great game in the already outstanding decade of the 1970s. Both teams had good records, and yet another Cardinal Conference Championship was on the line. The year 1978 also saw New Phila snap a four-year winless streak against its rivals and the final rivalry game for Dover head coach Tom Redman.

Coming into the seventy-fourth renewal of the rivalry, both Dover and New Phila had already had outstanding seasons. Dover in 1978 was led by many talented players on offense. Dover's star running back, Ken Rufener, had put together a very nice season, rushing for 864 yards coming into the big game. Even better than Dover's rushing attack was its ability to put the ball in the air. Led by talented receivers Robbie Woods, Eric Redman, Kenny Grove and tight end Steve Kopec, quarterback Jeff Mamarella had

The 1978 New Philadelphia High School football team. *Courtesy of the Quaker Foundation.*

a plethora of targets. With all the talent on offense, it was no surprise that Dover came into the rivalry game with a record of 8-1.

Even when Mamarella went down in the fourth game of the year with a shoulder injury, Dover was prepared. The remainder of the 1978 season saw the emergence of Jamie Devore. With the help of his dynamite receivers, Devore would go on to an outstanding career as the Tornadoes' quarterback. In 1979, Devore would throw for 1,491 yards, thirteen touchdowns and the then single game record of 278 yards passing. Until the recent era of pass-first Dover teams, Devore held nearly every major passing record at the school.

On the Phila side, the Quakers were led by fourth-year head coach Jim Roman. Despite a very good record and a Cardinal Conference co-championship in 1975, he had never beaten Dover. The closest the Phila mentor had managed was a tie in 1976. That would all change in 1978, when Roman defeated Dover, earning the outright conference championship and the major-league bat for the very first time. After his victory in 1978, Roman would never again taste victory against his crosstown rival. Although his overall record at New Phila was a respectable 38-26-6, against Dover he was a dismal 1-5-1.

The Quaker team in 1978 was known more for its tough defense than for its offense. It was so good that the ten points Dover managed in losing were the most points the Quakers gave up in a game all season. On offense, the Quakers were led by running back Karl Beahm, fullback Ed Wilson and sophomore quarterback Steve Shade. Shade was definitely an anomaly on the 1978 team. He was one of only three underclassmen in the starting lineup. Coming into the big game, the Quakers were 7-1-1.

In what everyone expected to be a stalwart defensive game, it comes as a surprise that two touchdowns were scored in the very first period. First blood was drawn by the Quakers. Their sustained drive began at Dover's forty-six-yard line midway through the first quarter. The drive wasn't fancy, but it was effective. It featured the pounding running of backs Beahm and Wilson. The capper was an eleven-yard scamper by Beahm on a pitch to the right side. After the extra point, with 3:46 left in the first, New Phila led 7–0.

Dover's first score came in a much flashier style than that of the Quakers. Junior quarterback Jamie Devore connected on his first five passes, taking his Tornadoes down to Phila's twenty-six. Another big throw to Robbie Woods advanced the Tornado drive to the nine. With a first and goal at New Phila's nine, the Quaker defense tightened up. Dover got almost nothing on the next two plays, leaving them with third down and a long way to go to get to the Promised Land. Fittingly, Dover's score came on a pass. On third and goal, Devore dropped back and lofted a pass into the corner of the end zone. Tight end Steve Kopec pulled it in, and after the extra point, Dover had knotted the game, 7–7.

Unfortunately for Dover, Devore's good luck would not hold into the second quarter. Fairly deep in his own territory, Devore was picked off by New Phila's outstanding defender Rod Morrow. Morrow's interception was one of several great plays he would make that evening. The interception gave New Phila great field position at Dover's thirty-eight.

Again, the New Phila offense stuck to the ground game. It was spearheaded by fullback and eventual game MVP Ed Wilson. Wilson's one-yard plunge gave the home team a 13–7 lead. Surprisingly, instead of lining up for the extra point, New Phila's offense stayed on the field and attempted a two-point conversion. The botched try failed miserably when quarterback Steve Shade went one way and the offensive line went the other. After the game, Roman was asked about the play. He replied, "If you don't gamble once in awhile, you don't win the Dover-Phila game." The failed attempt left the Quakers ahead 13–7 with three minutes left in the half.

For the rest of the first half and well into the third quarter, the game became the defensive battle that most of the fans had expected coming in. Both teams failed to move the ball consistently. A continuing problem for Dover was its inability to run the ball. Despite his outstanding season, Ken Rufener would gain only seventeen yards on fourteen carries in the year's biggest game.

Two-thirds of the way through the third quarter, the offenses picked up when Phila drove all the way to the Dover twenty-one and looked primed to score. Dover's defense dug in its heels, forcing Phila into a fourth down situation. New Phila's young quarterback made a mistake, and the ball was picked off by Dover's Tim King. After a good return, Dover had first and ten at the thirty-nine-yard line. More importantly, it had a spark.

Dover's ensuing drive again featured precise passing and talented receivers. Kopec caught two passes, and Woods and Redman each caught one, accounting for forty-one yards. Although the drive stalled, Dover's kicker Ken Grove nailed a thirty-seven-yard field goal on fourth and eight. Although the ball just barely cleared the crossbar, it drew the Tornadoes to within three points. Roman's decision to go for two now meant that a field goal would tie the game.

It didn't take long for the Tornadoes to get back in business as New Philadelphia's Rod Morrow fumbled the kickoff. Dover's Don Gardner recovered at the eleven, and Dover looked sure to either tie the game or take the lead.

Rarely is a player able to redeem himself for a mistake, and even more rare is the opportunity presented almost immediately. For Rod Morrow, though, that was the case in 1978. On Dover's first pass attempt, Morrow barreled through the offensive line and tipped Devore's pass up in the air. Ed Wilson was the beneficiary of Morrow's hustle and of being in the right place at the right time. He intercepted the pass at the seven, and the Tornado opportunity was missed.

Dover would get two more chances to tie the game, but neither resulted in a score. The closest it came was halfway through the fourth quarter when it attempted a thirty-seven-yard field goal. This time, luck was not on the Tornadoes' side as the ball went short and left. The Quakers held the visitors once more before running out the clock to win the game and the Cardinal Conference Championship.

Following the game, New Phila's outstanding fullback Ed Wilson was named MVP. He rushed for a healthy ninety-five yards with a touchdown. Wilson was also a crucial piece of the puzzle on defense, with seven tackles and the big interception in the final seconds of the third quarter. The crucial interception was Wilson's fifth of the season.

Offensively, the Tornadoes were led by Devore, who threw twenty-two times, completing twelve passes for 109 yards and a touchdown. While Devore would be back in 1979 for another shot at the Quakers, head coach Tom Redman would not. Following the 1978 season, Redman left Dover to become the head coach at Lancaster High School.

1980: Dover, 9; New Phila, 7—A Game of Emotion

As hard as it is for diehard fans to admit, at times there are things that are more important than the game. At times it is also true that issues of emotion and life become intertwined with the game. The year 1980 was full

The Dover-Phila Football Rivalry

The 1980 Dover High School football team. *Courtesy of Denny Rubright.*

of emotions for both schools. One player from each school faced obstacles much greater than a goal line stand. They faced situations of life and death.

The 1980 football season was supposed to be Todd Espenschied's big opportunity. After sitting behind Dover's outstanding quarterback Jamie Devore, Espenschied had earned his chance. Unfortunately, life had different plans for the Dover senior. Instead of being a field general for the Tornadoes, Espenschied would be fighting cancer. Diagnosed with cancer of the knee and lung, he spent his final season as a Dover gridder undergoing chemotherapy. Immediately following the Dover-Phila game, he was scheduled to return to Columbus Children's Hospital for more treatment and surgery.

Steve Berentz also faced incredible obstacles his senior season. During a pre-season scrimmage, Berentz life changed forever when he was paralyzed. Although he would later pass away due to his injury, he was able to attend the rivalry game that year. For the trip, he was transported to the game by an ambulance on loan from the Meese-Bierie Funeral Home. Meese-Bierie provided the ride free of charge from Warren Hospital, where Berentz was undergoing paralysis therapy.

Perhaps the most emotional moment during that 1980 game took place during halftime while the teams were sequestered away in the locker room. In a special ceremony, Cleveland Browns head coach Sam Rutigliano

The Cardinal Conference Years

Pictured are New Philadelphia player Steve Berentz (left) and Dover player Todd Espenschied. Both players faced obstacles much greater than wins and losses, yet both provided inspiration to their teammates and their communities. *Courtesy of Denny Rubright.*

and sportscaster Jim Mueller helped present the boys and their families with checks for over $35,000 each. The money had been raised during a community-hosted telethon on local Channel TV-2. In addition, both the Dover and New Philadelphia firefighters worked together to "fill the boot" at the stadium gates, raising an additional $600 for the boys.

While the stories of Berentz, Espenschied and the support of their communities would be enough to make this a special game, there was also an excellent battle on the field in 1980. The game featured an underachieving Quaker team that had been picked to win a Cardinal Conference championship and perhaps score a playoff berth and a Dover team that had thoroughly exceeded expectations. The Tornadoes had lost almost everyone from an undefeated team in 1979. Despite several key injuries and a sophomore quarterback, the Dover team still managed a 7-1-1 record coming in with a tie against Steubenville and a last second loss to North Canton Hoover. The Hoover loss came on a "flea flicker" that cost the Tornadoes the game in week eight. On the field, the Tornadoes were led by quarterback Mike Bayer, who showed surprising poise despite his youth, and running backs Fred Todd, Mike Mencer and Steve Truchly. Dover was also blessed that year with outstanding line play. The line was anchored by Brian Burrell on both offense and defense and all-Ohio offensive tackle Craig Weiss.

New Philadelphia's team was talented but struggled to gel. For the first five games of the year, it was led by quarterback Steve Shade and running back Brian Timmerman. In week five, everything changed when Shade suffered a season-ending injury. Timmerman, a senior, sacrificed his position at running back and agreed to take over duties as the Quaker quarterback. To compliment Timmerman's running ability and fullback Mike Stokey, New Philadelphia installed an option-style offense. Coming into the big game, the change seemed to be working as the Quakers had won two of three to raise their record to 4-5.

On the sidelines, the Quakers were led by coach Jim Roman. Roman was in his fifth season as the Quaker mentor. During his tenure, Roman compiled an overall record of 38-26-6, including records of 8-1-1 in 1978 and 7-3 in 1979. After a second consecutive four-win season in 1981, he was not rehired to coach the team in 1982. Dover was led by first-year head coach Bob Maltarich. Coach Maltarich never had a losing season during his three years at Dover, going 24-6-1 before leaving Tuscarawas County for New Mexico State University in 1983. He spent three years at New Mexico State as an assistant before returning home to coach at West Holmes High School.

As Dover was favored to win by at least two touchdowns, the game was much closer than many believed it would be. Played at Quaker Stadium in front of a crowd of over ten thousand people, there was a great deal at stake for the Tornadoes. With a win, the Tornadoes would earn their second consecutive Cardinal Conference Championship and secure a playoff berth for the first time in school history. For their part, the Quakers had no aspirations of conference or playoff glory. Instead, their sole focus was ruining the Tornadoes' season and avenging a 28–7 loss in 1979.

The game began with both teams struggling to move the ball. This came as a surprise to a Tornado team that had powered to a season average of thirty points a game. That Friday night, the Quakers would hold them to a season-low nine points. It became quickly apparent that the Quakers had come to play. The team that Dover faced looked more like a 7-2 team than one with a record of 4-5.

The Cardinal Conference Years

The first big break of the game came when New Philadelphia fumbled a pitch. Most coaches will tell you that one of the biggest drawbacks to an option offense is the pitch. There's no telling what can happen when a live ball is repeatedly tossed out for the taking. On this particular play, Timmerman's pitch was fumbled and recovered by Dover's Rick Zuercher. With first and ten at the Quaker forty-five, the Tornadoes took advantage of the opportunity and drove down for the first score of the game. The points were on a twenty-three-yard field goal by Dover's kicker, Scott Heller, giving the Tornadoes a 3–0 lead.

Dover would threaten again later in the first half, but an ill-advised pass by Bayer was intercepted. The pick, by New Phila's Troy Maxwell at the New Philadelphia six-yard line, denied the Tornadoes another score. At halftime, the score remained 3–0 in favor of Dover. Riding an emotional high, the Quakers had shown their crosstown rivals that they had come to play.

Dover received the ball to start the second half and seemed to pick up where they left off. The offensive line was settling in, and the Tornado offensive machine was again able to move the pigskin. They drove into New Philadelphia territory but again were the victim of a costly turnover.

New Philadelphia took over and was able to move the ball to the Dover forty-yard line before the Tornado defense stiffened. It forced the Quakers into a third and twelve situation, setting up perhaps the most exciting play of the game. Facing another failed drive, Timmerman dropped back to pass. He found flanker Bob Richardson down the middle of the field for an electrifying forty-yard touchdown. After a successful extra point by Quaker kicker Rick Leggett, New Phila led the game 7–3 with a little over five minutes remaining in the third quarter.

Despite the surprise second half New Philadelphia lead, the Tornadoes didn't panic. Instead, they took the kickoff and set their ground game to work. Behind their strong offensive line play, the Tornadoes drove down the field eating up the clock. The drive ate up all but eleven seconds of the rest of the third quarter and was capped by a twenty-six-yard touchdown scamper by Dover's Fred Todd. A missed extra point made the score 9–7 in Dover's favor as the third quarter came to a close.

Taking over at the beginning of the fourth quarter, the Quakers were ineffective at moving the ball and faced a punting situation, but a controversial call on the punt would keep the drive alive. On the play, Dover's Steve

Truchly was whistled for making an illegal fair catch signal. While the call itself was borderline, the yardage penalty granted to the Quakers was clearly wrong. The ball was moved fifteen yards from the original line of scrimmage, giving the Quakers another shot with a first and ten. Later, it was revealed that the penalty should have been only five yards, which would not have been enough for the first down. Luckily, for the officials who blew the call, the Tornado defense would hold the Quakers and no harm would be done.

The remainder of the game was dominated by Dover's ball control offense. Taking over at its own seven, the Tornadoes drove well into Quaker territory before pinning the home team at its eighteen with a punt. Again, New Philadelphia was ineffective on offense, giving the Tornadoes the ball back with only 2:21 to play. Dover ran all but four seconds off the clock, winning the game 9–7.

Following the game, Dover's Steve Truchly was named MVP. Truchly rushed for fifty-two yards but also had nine tackles and two batted down passes. In addition to his work on the field, Truchly was kept quite busy during Dover-Phila week with his own business. Dover's 170-pound running back made a killing selling "Another One Bites the Tornado Dust" towels. During rivalry week alone, Truchly sold 288 towels. Playing off the Queen hit song, the towels were printed in Cleveland and sold by Truchly. As you might have guessed, a portion of the proceeds of the sales of the towels was donated to teammate Todd Espenschied.

1983: New Phila, 9; Dover, 7

The year 1983 marked an anomaly in the Dover-Phila rivalry. With the Quakers' hiring of 1957 graduate Ward Holdsworth in 1982, and the Tornadoes following suit by hiring John Marks, a 1968 Dover graduate, in 1983, the rivalry saw its first matchup of alumni head coaches.

In his second year as the Quaker head coach, Holdsworth had the boys playing up to his expectations. A 1957 graduate of New Philadelphia High School, Holdsworth played for the great Bill Kidd at a time when the Quakers dominated the rivalry. As a senior, Holdsworth helped the Phils demolish the Dover team in 1956. After college and before taking over at New Phila, Holdsworth had built his reputation at Newcomerstown, where

The Cardinal Conference Years

he posted a 79-48-3 record, including a 10-0 campaign in 1972. Hired to take over the Quakers in 1982, Holdsworth turned around the team going 7-3 and 8-2 in his first two years. One of the major changes made by coach Holdsworth was the introduction of the single wing offense. At the time New Phila began running the new offense, it was one of only a few teams in Ohio to do so. Holdsworth utilized the single wing to take advantage of his talent in the backfield. In many cases, the running back would take the direct snap from the center and execute the play much like a quarterback. Holdsworth would remain New Phila's head coach for a total of four seasons, compiling an overall record of 23-17. He stepped down following the 1985 season when the Quakers struggled to a 2-8 record.

Dover assistant coach John Marks was elevated to the head coaching position after Bob Maltarich moved on to New Mexico State University after the 1982 season. Marks served under three different head football coaches at Dover before being tapped for the top job. He came to the Tornadoes first in 1974, when he joined the staff as an assistant under coach Tom Redman. Despite Marks's deep ties to the school, he struggled as its head coach. Overall, he compiled a 17-23 record in four seasons and a 1-3 record against the team across the river.

The 1983 battle between the crosstown rivals was evenly matched with the Quakers coming in at 7-2 and Dover at 6-3. For once, the conference title was not on the line, as it had already been wrapped up by the Wooster Generals. What was on the line for both teams were bragging rights. This was especially important on the Quaker side, as they looked to end a four-year losing streak to the Tornadoes.

The Quakers in 1983 were led by their four team captains: Matt Dummermuth, Mark Bichsel, Brian Murphy and Blake Bailey. Helping the seniors was junior tailback Vince Miccichi, who would play an important role in New Phila's victory.

The Dover Tornadoes in 1983 were led by captains Ron Grimm and Brock Jones. Jones would go on to an outstanding career at the College of Wooster. While playing linebacker for the Fighting Scots, Jones was named a College All-American. Dover also featured outstanding kicker Mike Sudduth, quarterback Dave Pruni and half back Bryan Miller.

The seventy-ninth meeting between the two rivals was played at Dover's Crater Stadium in very poor conditions. Fans huddled under ponchos and umbrellas trying to escape a cold, soaking rain that sabotaged conditions on the field. Even under the circumstances, the Dover faithful still packed them in, with over sixty-five hundred turning out for the big game.

The game itself would be one of opportunities—opportunities that Dover failed to capitalize on, and those that New Philadelphia took advantage of. The first of these opportunities presented itself on Dover's very first drive. Held to fourth and one, the Tornadoes elected to punt. Dover's Heller lined up deep to receive the snap, but not deep enough. The wet ball sailed over his head and into the end zone. Faced with potentially setting up a Phila touchdown, Heller did the right thing and fell on the ball. The play gave the Quakers a 2–0 lead and what would be the eventual margin of victory.

Following the blown punt snap, neither team was able to move the ball on offense for the rest of the first quarter and well into the second. That all changed, though, when New Phila took over and began to drive with a little less than four minutes to go before the half. The Quakers ripped off a seventy-three-yard scoring drive, starting at their own twenty-seven. Despite the poor weather, all the big plays in the drive were passes, a fourteen-yarder to Mike Demattio and two completions to Matt Dummermuth for twenty-eight and nineteen yards, respectively.

Dummermuth's nineteen-yard catch, resulting in the game's first offensive score, came on a broken play. Instead of New Phila quarterback Dave Winston making the throw, the ball was snapped directly to tailback Vince Miccichi. Miccichi fumbled but was able to pick it up, set and throw, thanks to the strong offensive line play of the Red and Black. The Quaker tailback found Dummermuth in the left corner of the end zone for the big score. Behind a strong aerial attack, the Quakers held a 9–0 lead at halftime.

If the first half belonged to the Quakers, then the second half was owned by the Tornadoes. Despite this dominance, missed opportunities would hold them to only seven points. Beginning the half on fire, Dover fullback Brock Jones returned the opening kickoff out to the thirty-four-yard line. The offense took over, driving well into Quaker territory behind strong running and a twenty-three-yard catch by John Feutz. The Tornadoes looked primed to score at the New Phila sixteen when disaster struck. A Dover fumble ended the drive and gave the Quakers the ball back at their six-yard line.

Gaining the momentum, the Quakers mounted a potential scoring drive of their own in the third quarter. They drove all the way to Dover's red zone but were turned away. Hoping to put the game out of reach, the Quaker offense was intercepted by Steve Cox at the Tornado twelve, ending the threat.

Dover's lone scoring drive of the night came at the beginning of the fourth quarter. With their backs against the wall and the Quakers holding onto a 9–0 lead, the Tornado offense looked to make things interesting. Beginning at their own forty-one, Dover got things going quickly with a big play. After advancing to the forty-eight, Dover quarterback Dave Pruni found John Feutz on an out-and-up pattern. The ball sailed into Feutz's hands at the thirty, and he went the rest of the way to pay dirt untouched. A successful extra point made the game a very tight 9–7.

The defense stepped up on the next possession, and the Tornadoes had a real chance, down by only two, with four minutes to play and an excellent kicker. Taking over at their own forty-four, the Tornadoes looked poised to score and steal one from the Quakers after a thirty-three-yard pass from Dave Pruni to Mike Sudduth. The big gainer took the Tornadoes all the way to the Quaker twelve. Jubilation quickly turned to disappointment, though, as a flag was spotted back at the line of scrimmage. Dover had executed an illegal shift before the snap, and Sudduth's big catch would go for nothing.

After the penalty, Dover was never able to regain the momentum. On fourth down, Pruni was dragged down for a sack, and the Quakers took over possession. With just seconds remaining, New Phila fell on the ball to end the game. In a matchup this close, it comes down to how the ball bounces. In a game that either team could have won, the breaks went to the New Philadelphia Quakers.

1984: New Phila, 7; Dover, 6

For those lucky enough to be part of the Dover-Phila rivalry during the first half of the 1980s, they saw perhaps one of the most competitive periods in the one hundred–plus years. A total of twenty-three points separated the teams in the six games between 1980 and 1985. Included in this stretch was a 14–0 shutout in 1981. If one class of seniors can be said to have been part of the most exciting stretch in the rivalry's history, it would probably be the class of 1986. In that class's three games in the fall of 1983, 1984 and 1985, a total of only four points separated the rivals.

The Dover-Phila Football Rivalry

The 1984 New Philadelphia High School football team. *Courtesy of the Quaker Foundation.*

The middle year of this stretch is perhaps the best game of the three, although it may also have been the sloppiest. For the 1984 contest, emotions were running even higher than usual. In the week leading up to the game, New Philadelphia High School was badly vandalized, resulting in added tension between the rival schools. Although the investigation would later find that Dover students had nothing to do with the break-in, at the time, many incorrectly assumed that Dover students had been responsible. Adding to the hype of the upcoming game was the fact that both teams came into the game on matching winning streaks of three games. Both teams also sported identical 5-4 records. The contest's winner would finish a respectable 6-4, while the loser would drop to a disappointing 5-5.

Returning to the sidelines for Dover, in his second year, was head coach John Marks. After a 6-4 first year, Marks again had his team in position to match that mark. A win would also avenge a 9–7 loss to the Quakers in 1983. Leading the charge for the Tornadoes was senior tailback Bryan Miller. The speedy Miller had earned a well-deserved reputation in the Tuscarawas Valley for his big play capabilities. New Phila knew that to stop the Tornadoes, it would have to contain Miller. In addition to Miller, the Tornado backfield featured quarterback John Feutz, fullback Chris Bitikofer and tight end Ryan Armstrong. Armstrong came from one of Dover's great football families. His grandfather, Tom Armstrong, served as an assistant coach for twenty-two years, and his father, Tom Armstrong Jr., did the same for twenty-seven seasons of his own.

The Cardinal Conference Years

For the Quakers, Ward Holdsworth returned to coach the team in his third season at the New Phila helm. Holdsworth was looking to go 6-4 for the year to complement his records of 7-3 and 8-2 in 1982 and 1983, respectively. The 1984 Dover-Phila game also held an extra special significance for Holdsworth. If he could beat his crosstown rival, he would win his 100th game as a head coach. Included in this total was his record of 79-48-3 at Newcomerstown and his three years as the head coach of the Quakers. Leading the charge for Holdsworth's 100th win and for New Phila's second straight win against the Tornadoes was tailback extraordinaire Vince Miccichi. In 1984, Miccichi was crucial to the Quakers' success as a team. Although no one player will carry a team to victory in football, Miccichi came close. Of the Quakers' five wins coming into the showdown with the Tornadoes, their three-game winning streak came only after Miccichi returned from injury in week six. During those three games, Miccichi not only ran the Quakers to victory, but he passed as well. In three games, six times he hooked up with wingback Dan Reinhart on touchdown passes. In only five starts, Miccichi accounted for 250 yards rushing and 668 yards through the air. Joining Miccichi on the Quaker offense was senior fullback Craig Steele, who was the team's leading rusher.

Nearly eight thousand fans came out for the game at Quaker Stadium hoping to see a great game. What they were treated to for the first three quarters was a sloppy, poorly played mess. Neither team was able to do much with the ball, as turnovers were commonplace. In the first quarter and a half, New Philadelphia managed a fumble and two interceptions, while the Tornadoes handed the ball back to their rivals twice with a fumble and an interception of their own.

Even with a plethora of turnovers, both teams did have their opportunities. On only the second play of the game, Dover looked to be in business when Jeff Fickes recovered a New Phila fumble on the Quaker twenty-six-yard line. Dover took the turnover and advanced down to the Quaker thirteen behind the strong running of Miller, but an interception stopped the drive cold.

Dover would get another opportunity at the end of the first quarter, but again a costly turnover ended the drive. Moving well into Quaker territory, Dover reached the twenty-eight-yard line. Unfortunately for the Tornadoes, a fumble put a stop to their scoring opportunity. The game would go to the half tied at 0–0.

The Dover-Phila Football Rivalry

The second half started much like the first had ended, with both teams unable to move the ball, but on Dover's second possession of the half, it began to have success. It drove deep into Phila territory before a timely sack by the Quakers forced a fourth down. On the play, Dover quarterback John Feutz dropped back to pass from the New Phila thirteen but was taken down for a seven-yard loss. Hoping to get the lead and put some points on the board, Coach Marks opted to go for a field goal on fourth down, but the thirty-seven-yard kick sailed wide right and short. Despite moving the ball, the Tornadoes had nothing to show for it.

Beginning at the end of the third quarter, Dover was finally able to capitalize on a drive and score the game's first points. The Tornadoes moved the ball forty-seven yards on eight running plays to take the lead. Carrying the load for Dover were Miller and quarterback John Feutz. Throughout the drive, the Tornadoes were never forced to put the ball in the air. The scoring play was a dynamic six-yard sweep by Miller. Looking as if he would be stopped short, Miller went airborne at the two-yard line and crashed into the end zone for the score. Although the extra point attempt failed, Dover led 6–0 with 11:38 remaining to play in the game.

With Dover taking the lead, things looked bleak for the New Phila Quakers. In the first three quarters combined, they had managed only three first downs and had never held the ball for more than six consecutive plays. That all changed, though, after the Tornadoes scored. Dover's lead seemed to wake up the New Phila offense as Vince Miccichi went to work. New Phila put together its first sustained drive behind the passing and running of Miccichi. The Quakers drove to Dover's twelve, where Miccichi lofted a pass toward the end zone. Unfortunately for the Quaker star, it fell just short and was intercepted by Fickes at the one-yard line. Although they didn't come away with points, the Quakers now knew they could move the ball on the tough Dover defense.

After an unsuccessful drive and punt by the Tornadoes, the Quakers had another shot with 4:09 remaining in the game. Beginning at Dover's forty-eight-yard line, the Quakers mounted what would be the game-winning drive. Taking advantage of a pass interference call that took the Quakers down to Dover's thirty-three, the Red and Black put together an eight-play drive that was capped by a nine-yard pass from Miccichi to Eric Ricklic with only 1:15 to go. The extra point by kicker junior Tim Labus gave the Quakers a one-point lead, 7–6.

The Cardinal Conference Years

Getting the ball back with just over a minute left, Dover didn't panic. They moved the ball to midfield before disaster struck when Feutz was intercepted with less than thirty seconds to play. The interception was returned to Dover's thirty-eight. With only twenty-one seconds left, the game was nearly over. Fortunately for the Tornadoes, they had all of their timeouts left, and miraculously they would hold the Quakers and actually get the ball back.

With only four seconds remaining in the game, the Tornadoes had one last shot. Those four seconds would provide one of the oddest endings in the rivalry's history. Beginning at its own thirty-seven, Dover took to the air. Its first pass attempt fell incomplete, and only one tick remained on the clock. On what should have been the game's final play, Feutz took the snap and was forced to scamper out to the Quaker forty-two before he was tackled. No time remained on the clock. The problem for the Red and Black was that amidst all the celebration, there was a flag down. The Quaker fans, in their jubilation, were too impatient to wait until the play ended before storming the field. Because a game could not end on a penalty, Dover would get another shot.

It took nearly ten minutes, but eventually the fans were removed from the field and the penalty was assessed. When the dust cleared, it appeared that Dover had a real shot to alter the outcome. The Tornadoes would attempt a forty-four-yard field goal that could potentially silence the overzealous Quaker throng and truly steal the game. Alas, it wasn't to be. New Phila linebacker Sam Shook became an instant hero as he burst through the line to block the game-winning attempt. Without a flag on the field, the Quaker players and fans were free to celebrate one of the rivalry's most exciting finishes.

The MVP of the 1984 game went to its most hyped player and 1983 MVP Vince Miccichi. Miccichi rushed for forty-four yards and passed for seventy-eight. More importantly, he threw the game-winning touchdown pass to Ricklic with a little over a minute remaining. Leading the way for the Tornadoes was tailback Bryan Miller, who finished the game with 112 yards rushing and Dover's lone touchdown.

1989: Dover, 28; New Phila, 22—The Comeback

Many times, a football game can become a tale of two halves. The 1989 rivalry game is a great example of this. The contest featured a dominant New Phila team in the first half and a rejuvenated Dover team in the second. With playoff implications for Dover and a ninety-four-yard fumble return for a touchdown thrown in for good measure, 1989 was truly a memorable year.

New Phila's team in 1989 had struggled despite some good talent in the backfield. They featured senior fullback Shawn Gribble and senior quarterback Gabe Richmond. Even with his team's offensive struggles, Gribble had amassed 717 yards and eight touchdowns coming into the contest. Coming into the Dover-Phila game, the Quakers had lost four of five and had been shut out in three of their nine games. With the exception of a forty-one-point outburst against Canton South, the Quakers had struggled to average ten points per contest.

Leading the charge from the sidelines was coach Dan Evans. Evans was born in Barnesville, Ohio, and attended high school at Cambridge. After graduating from Cambridge in 1963, he attended West Liberty College. Evans's coaching experience included stints at West Holmes, where he compiled a record of 29-19-2, and Findlay High School, where he coached for two years. Evans was chosen from forty-seven candidates to become the new Quaker coach after the resignation of Ward Holdsworth. Beginning in 1986, he would coach the Red and Black for four seasons, compiling a record of 19-21 as head coach. Evans resigned after a tough 1989 season.

Coaching the Dover Tornadoes in his first year was alumni Jeff Souers. Souers was an outstanding running back for the Crimson and Gray in the mid-1960s under coach Dick Haines. After graduating from Dover, Souers attended Southern Illinois University and later Capital University, where he graduated in 1971. His coaching career began as an assistant at Wooster, before he got his first opportunity to be a head coach at Waynedale High School from 1977 to 1985. From Waynedale, Souers headed to Maple Heights High School for three seasons before returning to his alma mater. In six seasons as Dover's head coach, Souers compiled a record of 32-29 with outstanding seasons in 1989 (7-4) with a playoff appearance, 1990 (8-2) and 1993 (7-3).

Coming into the big game in 1989, the Tornadoes were enjoying a great deal of success under Souers with a 6-3 record and a shot at the playoffs

The Cardinal Conference Years

The 1989 Dover High School football team. *Courtesy of Denny Rubright.*

if they could beat the Quakers. They were led by seventeen seniors at the twenty-two starting positions, including captains and starting tackles Todd Holt and Ron Schweitzer. These two big guys up front had gotten really good at opening up holes for Dover's tough but undersized fullback Jim Stock. Coming into the 1989 season, Stock was simply hoping to find his name on the first team roster. At five-foot-seven and about 170 pounds, Stock was not your prototypical bruising fullback, but he had toughness and heart. Through nine games, he had put up very respectable numbers, with 753 yards and ten touchdowns.

The eighty-fifth clash between the crosstown rivals was played in near perfect conditions at Crater Stadium. A capacity crowd came out to cheer on their teams with temps in the mid-sixties and not a drop of rain in sight. Unfortunately for the hometown fans, they didn't have much to cheer for early on. New Phila came out blistering hot. In the first quarter alone, Shawn Gribble rushed for 137 yards and two touchdowns. Gribble's two short plunges of 2 and 1 yard(s) in the first gave the Quakers a quick 14–0 lead. Not bad for a team that had trouble scoring all season. The offense that arrived at Crater Stadium on that warm November night looked nothing like the team that had lost four of five games. On that night, the Quaker offense would rack up 541 yards of total offense, with Gribble leading the way rushing for 224 yards.

Down 14–0 in the second period, the Tornado offense came alive. Led by the tough running of Stock and the play of quarterback Damon Stevenson, Dover marched down the field to score with 8:27 left in the second. The touchdown came on a one-yard burst by Stock. It would be the first of three on that night for the Dover senior. After a Quaker penalty drew them closer to the goal line, Dover coach Jeff Souers took a risk and went for the two-point conversion. Luckily for Souers, he had the fleet-footed Stevenson, who trotted in for the two points. This two-point conversion would come back to haunt the Quakers later in the game.

As if in response to the Tornado score, New Phila proved yet again that the first half belonged to it. Capped by a twelve-yard run by senior quarterback Gabe Richmond, the Quakers widened the gap to 20–8. Here things got interesting as New Phila decided to try and match Dover's two-point conversion with one of its own. The attempt was stuffed, and the score remained 20–8 and would through halftime.

If Phila owned the first half, then Dover can claim rights to the second. This is especially true with the costly turnovers that prevented a Quaker win. Quite possibly, the turning point of the game came late in the third quarter when New Phila drove to Dover's four-yard line. Facing fourth and one, a Quaker first down would give them four tries at the end zone from three yards out and the opportunity to go up 27–8. It wasn't to be, though, as Dover's defense stopped Shawn Gribble six inches short of the first, giving the ball back to the Tornadoes.

The Tornado drive that began at their own four-yard line was a complete reversal of fortune. The Crimson and Gray marched its offense ninety-six yards in eleven plays to pull within 20–14. The touchdown again came from fullback Jim Stock from five yards out. Although Jones's kick was no good, the Tornadoes now only trailed 20–14. They could take the lead with a touchdown and extra point.

When the Quakers got the ball back, it didn't take long for disaster to strike. Dover's Kip McDade intercepted a Gabe Richmond pass at the Quaker forty-five to put Dover back on offense. With just under nine minutes remaining in the game, the Quakers now faced a Dover team with momentum and field position, all the while they were stuck clinging to a six-point lead.

With the Tornadoes driving, the worst-case scenario unfolded for the Quakers. The Crimson and Gray needed only six plays to cover the forty-five yards and score the go-ahead touchdown. The big play was again provided by Dover's McDade, who made an acrobatic catch on a pass from Stevenson. The completion netted the Tornadoes thirty-nine yards and took

The Cardinal Conference Years

their offense all the way down to the Quaker seven-yard line. Just a few short plays later, Stock bullied his way across the Quaker goal line to tie the game. Jones's kick was good, and Dover had its first lead of the ball game, 21–20.

If one thing can be said for the Quakers that night, it is that they never quit. Facing Dover's remarkable comeback, the Quakers went back to work and drove immediately down the field on the Tornado defense. With just six minutes remaining in the game, the Quakers reached the Dover eight-yard line. The biggest play of the drive was provided by Gabe Richmond, who hooked up with Dan Mamula for a twenty-four-yard completion.

Once they were on the eight, the Dover defense tightened up, forcing the Red and Black into a crucial fourth and one. This time, Shawn Gribble wouldn't be denied. New Phila picked up the first and looked primed to score the potential game-winning touchdown. That was when one of the oddest and most exciting plays in the 110-year history of the rivalry happened.

On first and goal, New Phila quarterback Gabe Richmond handed off the ball to Shawn Gribble, who powered toward the line. Rushing like a freight train, Gribble was met by Eric Pfeiffer. Pfeiffer put a bone-crushing hit on

Pictured is Dover's Don Watson. With a little less than three minutes remaining in the 1989 rivalry game, Watson pulled off one of the most unlikely touchdowns in the game's 110-year history. *Courtesy of Denny Rubright.*

the Quaker back, getting his helmet on the pigskin and popping it loose. Like a Hollywood movie script, the ball landed squarely in the hands of Dover defensive end Don Watson. Although Watson will never be confused for Carl Lewis, he rumbled, bumbled and stumbled his way ninety-four yards for a Dover touchdown. Led by a slew of blockers, Watson was never in serious danger of being tackled. This stunning turn of events put the Tornadoes on top, at 28–20, with only 2:32 remaining in the game.

Again, the New Phila Quakers refused to quit. Two big passes from Richmond to Bruce Vandall, after the kickoff, had the Quakers threatening. The completions for fifty-five and twenty-five yards came on consecutive plays and took the New Phila team all the way to Dover's five-yard line. On first down, Richmond carried to the two, giving the Quakers second and goal on the two-yard line. Sadly for the visitors, the next play ended any real hopes they had of upstaging Dover's two-touchdown comeback. On the play, Richmond dropped back and appeared to have Vandall open for the touchdown. Instead, Dover defensive back and quarterback Damon Stevenson picked off the pass, ending the scoring threat. New Phila had come so close in the second half, but costly turnovers deep in Dover's territory were its undoing.

Pinned deep within Quaker territory, Dover was unable to do anything with the ball but run a little time off the clock. On fourth down, not wanting to risk a blocked punt, the Tornadoes took an intentional safety to make the score 28–22. Although New Phila would get to run one play after the free kick, a desperation throw from Richmond to Vandall fell incomplete, and the Tornadoes won the game.

The 1989 game saw many outstanding performances on both sides of the ball, but three really stand out as game changers. New Phila's Shawn Gribble was the heart of the Quaker offense in the losing effort. On that night, he rushed for 224 yards on thirty-six carries. He also scored two of New Phila's three touchdowns. For Dover, the offense was led by senior and game MVP Jim Stock, who finished the night with 142 yards on twenty-eight carries and three touchdowns. While the big stats went to the two running backs, perhaps no one came up bigger than Dover's defensive hero Kip McDade. McDade anchored the Dover defense, had a key interception and made an acrobatic catch for thirty-nine yards.

5
THE MODERN ERA
1990–2010

1992: DOVER, 17; NEW PHILA, 14

Coming into the matchup between Dover and New Philadelphia in 1992, some people had begun to question the importance of the game. Many argued that without the two teams playing in the same conference, the game simply didn't mean as much as it had in the past. Not helping the cause were two New Phila blowouts of the Tornadoes in 1990 and 1991 and several seasons of subpar records for both teams. Some people even went so far as to question whether Dover-Phila remained the best rivalry in Tuscarawas County. After 1992, the questions all went away. That year, the two teams, with their entire seasons riding on one game, left everything on the field in one of the rivalry's greatest games.

To most local football experts, the Dover-Phila game in 1992 should not have been one to make a book like this. Coming into the game, both teams sported losing records, with Dover at 2-7 and New Phila at 3-6 in the very tough Federal League. That year, the two teams shared only one opponent: the Claymont Mustangs. While Dover fell to Claymont 21–6, the Quakers beat it 23–14. In addition to the common opponent, Dover's senior class of 1993 had never defeated the Quakers on the football field. At all levels, from freshman on up, these Tornadoes were winless against their crosstown rivals. All of these factors combined led to a heavily favored New Phila team.

The Dover-Phila Football Rivalry

The 1992 Dover High School football team. Courtesy of Denny Rubright.

New Phila's coach, Les Wojciechowski, was returning for his second year, having bested the Tornadoes the previous year by a score of 38–14. Wojo, as he was nicknamed, had come to New Philadelphia in 1988 as an assistant under Dan Evans. When Evans left, Wojo stayed on and worked under head coach Joe Tressey in 1990 before being elevated to the head job in May 1991. Coach Wojciechowski would only remain the Quaker coach for two years before resigning to return to Evans's staff as an assistant at Cambridge. His overall record as the Quaker head coach was 7-13.

Anchoring Wojo's 1992 Quakers was outstanding running back Chris Perkins. Despite the tough schedule against schools like Jackson, Perry, Glen Oak and North Canton, Perkins came into the Dover-Phila game needing only 32 yards to become the first Quaker rusher to crack 1,000 yards in twenty-one years. Also in New Phila's backfield was senior quarterback Eric Williams. That season, Williams had thrown for 526 yards and rushed for an additional 188. On defense, the Quakers were led by linebacker Jacob Powell, who came into the game with fifty-nine tackles, two and a half sacks and three forced fumbles.

For Dover, head coach Jeff Souers returned in his fourth season as the Tornado mentor. The year 1992 was a trying one for Souers as injuries and turnovers haunted the boys in Crimson and Gray. One positive to come out of the injuries was the valuable experience gained by some of the Tornado underclassmen. Of the twenty-two starting spots, thirteen were held by underclassmen, including five sophomores in the starting lineup and a sophomore kicker. It would be the play of these young Tornadoes that would propel the team to an unlikely victory. The statistical leaders for the Tornadoes in 1992 were running back Marty Kail, with 357 yards, and sophomore quarterback Brent Morrison, with 347 yards and two touchdowns

The Modern Era

through the air. Defensively, the Tornadoes were led by a pair of talented juniors—Jason Wallick at linebacker and Alex Sica on the defensive line.

The 1992 edition of the rivalry was played in front of sixty-five hundred people on a cold November night at Quaker Stadium. At game time, the temperature hovered in the mid-twenties with overcast skies. Despite the chilly temperatures, Dover came out fired up. Junior Jason Wallick broke off a nice return to start the game, and the Tornado offense went to work at the Quaker forty-eight-yard line. The offense looked crisp, and before the fans could even settle into their seats, Dover had driven to New Phila's twenty-five.

Unfortunately for the Tornadoes, their old nemesis, the turnover, came calling when Brent Morrison was blindsided by a Quaker defender knocking the ball loose. New Phila's Richie Blade recovered, and the Dover threat was over. Taking advantage of the opportunity, the Quakers marched sixty-four yards on sixteen plays to take a 7–0 lead. Senior Chris Perkins carried most of the load and was rewarded with the touchdown from one yard out. Marc Cobane's extra kick made the score 7–0 with only a few ticks left in the first quarter.

After returning the kickoff to the twenty-five-yard line, Dover was back in scoring territory quickly, thanks to one of its starting sophomores. On the first play of the second quarter, running back Matt Lautzenheiser broke a delay draw, scampering sixty-seven yards before fellow sophomore Randy Noah could pull him down at the eight-yard line. Riding high on the momentum, Kail bulled his way through into the end zone on fourth and two. Sophomore kicker Scott Blind's extra point knotted the score at 7–7, where it would remain until halftime.

The start of the second half showed that both teams could move the ball, yet neither seemed to be able to get over the hump and score. New Phila drove to Dover's thirty-seven and was forced to punt, and Dover drove to the New Phila eleven but turned over the ball on downs. The first break of the second half for the Tornadoes came when their crosstown rivals fumbled and Dover's Scott Harmon recovered at the Quaker sixteen. A personal foul penalty took the ball down to the eight, where Morrison found Kail on an eight-yard completion to take the lead. Blind's kick made the score 14–7 with less than a quarter to play.

New Phila took the kickoff without much success, and it looked like the Tornadoes had the momentum. Quaker quarterback Eric Williams was sacked on consecutive plays, forcing a third and fourteen deep in his own territory. In desperate need of a first down and a big play, New Phila got that and more from speedy tailback Chris Perkins. On a well-executed screen pass, Williams found Perkins, who raced down the sideline for a seventy-five-yard touchdown. Just like that, the Quakers were back in the game. Cobane's kick tied the score at 14–14.

In the middle of the quarter, both teams failed to move the ball as they exchanged punts. A good Phila punt pinned the Tornadoes at their thirty with less than five minutes to play. Undeterred, Dover drove down the field, with the big play coming on a seventeen-yard completion from Morrison to Kail. With the ball spotted on the New Phila seven-yard line, the Tornadoes looked primed to score, but the Quakers would not give in so easy. Morrison was sacked, pushing the ball back to the eighteen. On second down from the eighteen, Kail was stuffed, and both teams were penalized for unsportsmanlike behavior. When the dust settled, Dover had third and goal at the twelve. Here, Morrison made one of the best decisions of the night. Forced from the pocket, the young quarterback was able to get rid of the ball instead of either taking a sack or throwing into coverage. The decision kept the ball at the twelve and gave Dover a shot at a game-winning field goal.

With only twenty-five seconds remaining in a deadlocked football game, Dover's sophomore kicker trotted onto the field. In the game, Blind was two for two on extra points but had not attempted a field goal. For the season, he was one for two on field goal attempts, with a successful effort against Carrollton and a miss against Cambridge. The missed field goal against Cambridge would have won the game for the Tornadoes. Now, with just seconds remaining in the biggest game on the schedule, Blind had a chance at redemption. After timeouts from both sides, the ball was finally snapped and placed perfectly by holder Kevin Miller. Blind connected cleanly with the ball and watched as it sailed right down the middle from thirty yards out.

With only seconds remaining in the game, the underdog Tornadoes held on to win, giving the senior class its first ever victory over the Quakers. Despite the disappointing outcome, several Quaker players did put together outstanding games. Senior running back Chris Perkins got his 32 yards and more, to finish the game with 115 yards rushing and two touchdowns. The performance made him the first Quaker to rush for 1,000 yards in twenty-one years. On defense, the Quakers were led by junior Dave Wright, who

The Modern Era

had nine tackles and a sack. Leading the way for the Tornadoes was game MVP Marty Kail. Kail rushed for 70 yards, caught two passes for 43 yards and scored both Tornado touchdowns. On defense, the Tornadoes were led by Jason Celce. Celce played the greatest game of his high school career in helping the Dover defense stifle the Quakers.

DAN IFFT USHERS IN A NEW ERA OF DOVER FOOTBALL

On April 9, 1995, Dan Ifft was selected as Dover's twenty-fourth head football coach. At the time of his hiring, Ifft was thirty-eight years old and had never been a head coach at the high school level. Sixteen years later, he has become Dover's winningest head coach, transforming the program into a perennial power.

Dan Ifft attended Warren JFK High School in the Youngstown area, where he excelled as a high school athlete in both track and football, finishing fourth at the state track meet in the 120-meter high hurdles. As a teenager, Ifft aspired to be an attorney, but while at Kent State University, his love of teaching and coaching won over his desire to practice law. Graduating in 1978 with his bachelor's degree, Ifft was hired by Austintown Fitch High School, where he served as an assistant football coach from 1979 to 1982. From Fitch, Ifft moved to Stark County, where he joined the staff of coach Keith Wakefield. Ifft would coach at Massillon Perry from 1983 to 1984 and 1986 to 1994. In

Dover coach Dan Ifft. *Courtesy of Mitchell's Studio.*

1985, while working toward his master's degree in sports administration, Coach Ifft worked as a graduate assistant with the Kent State University football team.

Content to work under coach Wakefield, Ifft only applied for the Dover job on a whim. His interviews went very well, and Ifft quickly impressed with his philosophy on coaching and winning. At the conclusion of the interview process, Ifft was selected from the fifty candidates for the job. Among those who applied were former Dover coach Bob Maltarich and Zanesville mentor Whit Parks.

Upon taking over the program, Ifft immediately sought to place a renewed emphasis on the football program. Several up and down years for the Tornadoes had caused numbers to dwindle along with the enthusiasm. The first step toward reinventing the program was an overhaul of the Crater Stadium facilities. This included a makeover of the home locker room and a reorganization of the weight room. Coach Ifft also began to increase the expectations on his team through mandatory 6:00 a.m. workouts. Having workouts before school allowed his athletes to still participate in other sports while continuing to foster a team feel with his football players.

In 1995, Coach Ifft led Dover to a 6-4 record and a victory over archrival New Philadelphia, 14–0. The following year, the team went 9-1 and brought home its first conference championship since 1982. Success bred more success, and Coach Ifft has now become Dover's winningest coach.

By 1999, Ifft's culture of winning had produced his first undefeated team. Led by Dover's all-time leading rusher, Colby Byrom, the team was also Tuscarawas County's first ever team to win a state playoff game. Under Coach Ifft, Dover has never suffered a losing record.

Probably the coach's greatest attribute is his adaptability. Dover has used a variety of different offenses during Ifft's tenure as coach. Each one was chosen because it complemented the talent that Dover featured in a given year. Whether it was the run-first offense that was propelled by Byrom and Zack Daley or the pass-first offense that has become commonplace in recent years, Dover refuses to be predictable. The best example of this is the Tornadoes' switch to a spread offense in 2002. Taking advantage of the strong arm of quarterback Todd Lisowski, Dover's offense put up impressive numbers in 2002 and 2003. During his senior season, Lisowski threw for 3,098 yards and eighteen touchdowns. Lisowski was twice named the Dover-Phila game MVP, going 2-0 against the Quakers as a starter.

The Modern Era

While the record that Coach Ifft has amassed at Dover is impressive, nothing has endeared him to Dover fans more than his dominance of the New Phila Quakers. Against the Red and Black, Ifft sports a record of 15-2, with one of those wins coming 45–0 in the state football playoffs. While at Dover, Ifft's teams have outscored the Quakers a whopping 539–159. Also during Ifft's tenure, the Tornadoes have regained the series lead. When Dover defeated the Quakers twice in 2008, it held the lead in the all-time series for the first time ever.

1996: Dover, 7; New Phila, 6

Although the 1996 contest between the Dover Tornadoes and the New Philadelphia Quakers was only the 92nd in the series' long history, it does hold the special distinction of marking the 100th anniversary of the first time the schools squared off. Although the teams came in with very different records, the game befitted the honor of being the 100th. Great defensive play, spectacular players and a fourth quarter victory make this one of the best games of the 1990s.

Leading the Quakers in 1996 was second-year head coach Claude Brown. Brown first arrived in New Phila as an assistant to head coach Phil Mauro. When Mauro left the Quakers to coach Massillon Jackson in 1995, Brown was hired to replace him. Brown was well liked by his players, who petitioned the school board to have him hired after Mauro's resignation. Just twenty-nine

The 1996 Dover High School football team. *Courtesy of Denny Rubright.*

when he became the Quaker head coach, Brown was a graduate of Canton McKinley High School, where he played on its 1981 State Championship team. Brown remained only two years at New Philadelphia, compiling a record of 5-15 overall and 0-2 against the Tornadoes.

Although New Philadelphia struggled to a record of 2-8 in 1996, it wasn't for a lack of talent on offense. The Quakers were led by three-year letterman and outstanding rusher J.J. Brindel and quarterback Cie Grant. Brindel would finish his career at New Phila with over thirty-two hundred yards for the Quakers. Grant is widely regarded as one of the most gifted athletes to come out of Tuscarawas County in decades. After a stellar career at New Phila, Grant attended the Ohio State University. While at Ohio State, he was a starter on the 2002 National Championship team. After college, Grant was drafted in the third round of the NFL draft by the New Orleans Saints.

Dover was led by head coach Dan Ifft in his second year for the Tornadoes. In his first year, Ifft took over a very young and inexperienced team, guiding them to a 6-4 record and a 14-0 victory over the Quakers. Ifft's 1996 team sat at 8-1 coming into the rivalry game, its only loss coming in the final minute against Triway when a sixty-six-yard pass ended the Tornadoes' chances at a perfect season. Leading the charge for Dover was senior quarterback Ryan Clugston and fellow senior and running back Tim McIlvaine.

Even though the teams came in with very different records, it was apparent early that the game would be much closer than many had predicted. The entire first half was a defensive battle between two tough clubs. New Phila's defense especially stepped up, holding the Tornadoes and their ball control offense to just five net yards in the half.

After a defensive stalemate in the first, New Phila shocked the Tornadoes by taking the lead in the second. The Quaker offense drove sixty-eight yards in thirteen plays to secure the game's first score. The big play of the drive was a scramble by agile quarterback Cie Grant for a twenty-four-yard gain. Capping the drive was New Phila's unsung hero, fullback Zach Espenschied. Espenschied bullied his way in from two yards out to give the Red and Black a 6–0 lead. With eight and a half minutes to play in the second, the score would remain 6–0 after a failed extra point. This missed extra point would come back to haunt the Quakers later. For the rest of the half, the defenses continued to play well, and the score remained the same.

The Modern Era

The second half began with Dover trying a little trickery with the opening kickoff. The play that Dover coach Dan Ifft later referred to as "rosebud" didn't work, and returner Tim McIlvaine was corralled at the sixteen-yard line. As if setting the tone, the Tornadoes continued to struggle with the ball, and at the end of three they found that their deficit remained 6–0.

Whether they wore down the defense or simply started executing better, we'll never know; either way, Dover's offense began to move the ball in the game's final frame. The Tornadoes would hold onto the ball for twenty-three plays in the fourth quarter while holding the Quakers, with Brindel and Grant, to only three offensive plays.

After a New Phila punt for a touchback to start the quarter, Dover took over with first and ten from its own twenty. On the very first play of the drive, Ryan Clugston hit Matt Ireland for a gain of twenty-four yards and Dover's first pass completion of the game. On the very next play, Clugston scrambled for another twelve yards, and the Tornadoes were in business at the Quaker forty-four. Twice during their fourth quarter scoring drive the Tornadoes were forced into a fourth down situation, and twice they came up big—once on a tough catch by Ireland and the second time on a crucial fourth down at the Quaker six.

On the second fourth down conversion, it looked as though Dover running back Tim McIlvaine was stopped for no gain, but a tough second effort pushed the gutsy runner over the first down marker. Just one play later, Clugston's pitch to the speedy Kevin Morris resulted in the Tornadoes' only score of the game. A successful kick by Steve Utter put Dover ahead by a score of 7–6.

With plenty of time left, the Quakers had an opportunity to pull ahead but could get nothing going on offense. A quick three and out and they were forced to punt the ball back to the Tornadoes. Dover wasn't about to give their archrivals another opportunity. Taking over at their own twenty, the Tornadoes' ball control offense went to work behind a great offensive line and the power running of backs Jason Garner and Tim McIlvaine. The Quakers would never get the ball back as Dover ran out the clock to win the game.

In hindsight, it was clearly the halftime adjustments by the Tornado coaching staff that led to the victory. The Dover offense accounted for all but five of their yards in the second half, and the defense held the Quakers without a first down in the final frame. Leading the way to a Dover victory were offensive stars Ryan Clugston (who took home MVP honors) and Tim McIlvaine. McIlvaine ground out eighty-one tough yards on twenty-three carries. Asked after the game, McIlvaine said he was just happy to finally play against the Quakers. In the two previous years, when the Dover runner was a sophomore and junior, he had been forced to sit out the big game with injuries. Also leading the way for Dover was two-way lineman Josh Renicker and senior inside linebacker Adam Donehue. Donehue recorded a game-high fourteen tackles.

1998: Dover, 66; New Phila, 21

Earlier in this book, you read about New Philadelphia's dominant victory in 1956. That win is still a source of pride for New Phila fans and embarrassment for those backing the Crimson and Gray. The same could also be said for the final three quarters of the 1998 rivalry game. For three quarters, the Dover Tornadoes scored at will on a helpless New Phila squad. There is

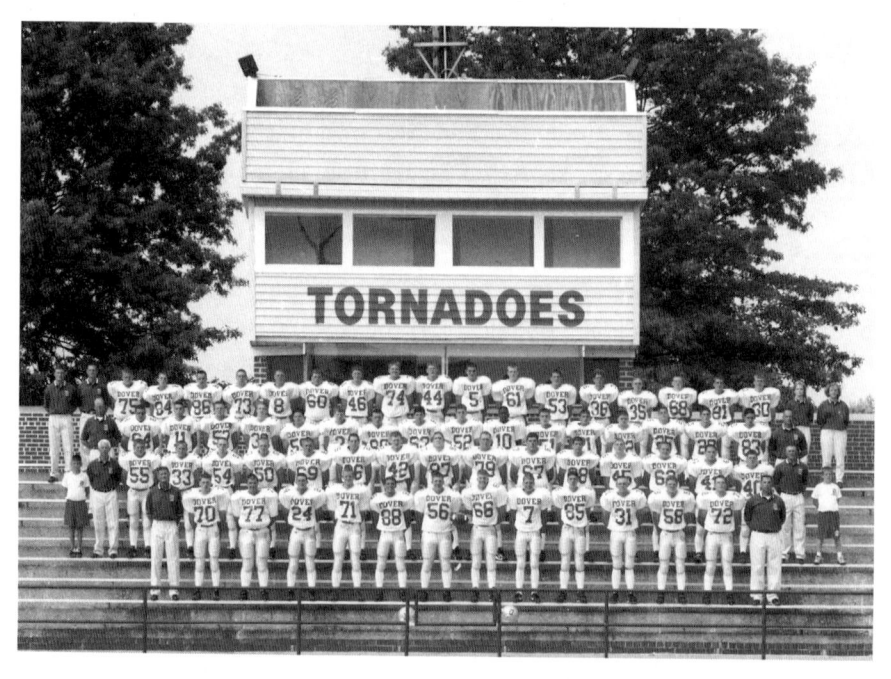

The 1998 Dover High School football team. *Courtesy of Mitchell's Studio.*

The Modern Era

one major difference between these two lopsided victories, though. Dover's domination was not total. In fact, it looked like the opposite would be true in the opening minute of the contest. At one point, the Quakers held a two-touchdown lead on the mighty Tornadoes. This stunning turnaround and the record-setting nature of this game make it memorable even if it wasn't a traditional "great" game.

The ninety-fourth matchup between the crosstown rivals was held on Friday, November 6, 1998. Coming into the game, both teams were playing well. The Tornadoes were red-hot, winning seven in a row, while New Philadelphia had won four of its last five after starting the season 1-3. Its win streak would have been five in a row if not for a tough loss (13–9) at the hands of Coshocton in week nine.

Coach Joe Studer's Quakers were led by a trio of talented running backs who helped them outscore their opponents 179–145. Sharing the load pretty equally were Greg Grant (128 carries for 903 yards), Todd Bracken (117 attempts for 551 yards) and fullback Chad Aubihl (588 yards on 104 carries). At quarterback for the Quakers was Chad Dorsey. Dorsey completed just over 50 percent of his passes on the year, for 566 yards.

While Phila's stats were respectable, especially the trio of running backs, Dover's were unbelievable. Dover coach Dan Ifft, in only his fourth season at the helm, had his Tornadoes scoring at a rate that was nearly unheard-of in rural Tuscarawas County. Coach Ifft's offense averaged a staggering thirty-six points per game. Better yet, it held an 8-1 record, a seven-game win streak and a ten-game win streak in the ECOL and was playing for its third straight conference championship and the opportunity to go to the playoffs.

On offense, the Tornadoes were led by the dynamic duo of senior Zack Daley, who had 740 yards on just 92 carries, and junior Colby Byrom, who had 1,125 rushing yards on 163 carries. The two running backs, Daley and Byrom, also had scored a whopping thirty-eight touchdowns combined. Byrom would go on to become Dover's all-time leading rusher, with stats that dwarfed any put up before or since. While the running backs were great, the real anchor to the Tornado offense that year was quarterback Marc Von Kaenel. Von Kaenel was a true on-field leader with a very good 1,270 yards passing, ten touchdowns and only three picks. All of these components, combined with a stingy Dover defense, made them an overwhelming favorite in the game. Unfortunately for the Tornadoes, someone forgot to tell New

The Dover-Phila Football Rivalry

Philadelphia that it was supposed to roll over and concede to the Tornadoes. Instead, the Quakers came out blistering hot, giving the Tornado faithful quite a scare in the opening moments of the game.

The game began unlike any game in the history of the rivalry. New Philadelphia put on a show, scoring fourteen points in the first 1:04 of the first quarter. In all, both Dover's defense and offense had been on the field for one play each before they found themselves down two scores. The scoring for the Quakers started from the very first play as New Phila's Ryan Range returned the game's opening kickoff eighty-seven yards for a touchdown. Stunned, Dover's offense took over deep in its own territory. On the very first play of the drive, quarterback and eventual game MVP Marc Von Kaenel had a pass picked off and returned to the Dover twelve-yard line by Greg Grant. Just one play later, fullback Chad Aubihl bulled his way into the end zone for the Quakers' second score of the game. Just like that, the Quakers had handed the favorites a big deficit.

Stuck in a 14–0 hole, the Dover offense again marched onto the field. This time, the Tornadoes were ready. On only the second play of the drive, senior Zack Daley put life back into the Tornadoes with an electrifying seventy-two-yard romp around the right end. Although he was dragged down at the two, the run stabilized the Tornado sideline. One play later, Byrom crossed the goal line, and the Tornadoes were down by a single score.

On New Phila's next possession, the magic seemed to have run out. Instead of making a big play to stun the Tornadoes yet again, the Quakers fumbled away the ball, setting up another score for the Tornadoes. The ball was stolen by Dover's Rob Becker and returned to the Quaker twenty-three. Just a few plays later, Von Kaenel found Bill Schumaker in the corner of the end zone for an eleven-yard touchdown to tie the game.

After failing to move the ball on the Tornadoes again, New Philadelphia's defense rallied to hold Dover to a Jeremy Compton field goal on their next possession. As time ticked down to end the first quarter, the score remained 17–14 in favor of Dover. To the fans, it looked like they might witness a classic shootout that November night. By halftime, it would be apparent that Dover was in complete control.

Building on the momentum of the last three drives, Dover surged to an offensive explosion in the second quarter. In just that one period, the Tornado offense scored four touchdowns to take a commanding 45–14 lead, sending many fans to the exits. In all, Dover would surge to fifty-nine unanswered points before the Quakers would get on the board again. Dover's offense looked unstoppable and its senior quarterback nearly perfect. Although Chad Aubihl would eventually break the consecutive point streak by the Tornadoes with six minutes left in the third period, the damage was already done and the game decided. Dover would tack on one more score in the fourth on a run by Von Kaenel to make the final 66–21.

While the game itself was not close after the second quarter, it is memorable and significant for the slew of records the teams set in the matchup. Like in New Phila's 1956 route, the margin of victory was Dover's greatest ever. In addition, the combined score was the highest ever in the rivalry game, with the two teams combining to score a remarkable four touchdowns in the first five minutes of the first quarter. While both Dover running backs had great games that evening—Daley had 138 yards rushing and 75 receiving and Byrom, 188 on the ground and 75 through the air—the real star of the game was Marc Von Kaenel. Von Kaenel threw for a whopping five touchdowns and ran for one more. His touchdown output in the game was half the total he had thrown for all season. In the end, some may argue with the inclusion of this game in the book. While not a close game, it certainly does qualify as memorable.

2004: New Phila, 21; Dover, 20—The 100th Game Exceeds All Expectations

Hollywood couldn't have written a better ending to the 2004 rivalry game between the Dover Tornadoes and New Philadelphia Quakers. After 99 games, unbelievably the series was all even at 45-45-9. Even better, the Quakers sat at 9-0 with a win over Dover giving them their first perfect season since 1944. Standing in the way of Quaker perfection was a 7-2 Dover team with a record nine game winning streak against their crosstown rival and a potential playoff berth riding on the outcome for the Tornadoes. Impossibly this game was as good as advertised with multiple lead changes and a one play win or go home scenario deciding the outcome. The 100th game was truly one for the ages.

Coming into the 100th matchup, the New Phila Quakers were on a roll. Undefeated in the season at 9-0, they had already clinched a share

The Dover-Phila Football Rivalry

2004 New Philadelphia High School football team. *Courtesy of Mitchell's Studio.*

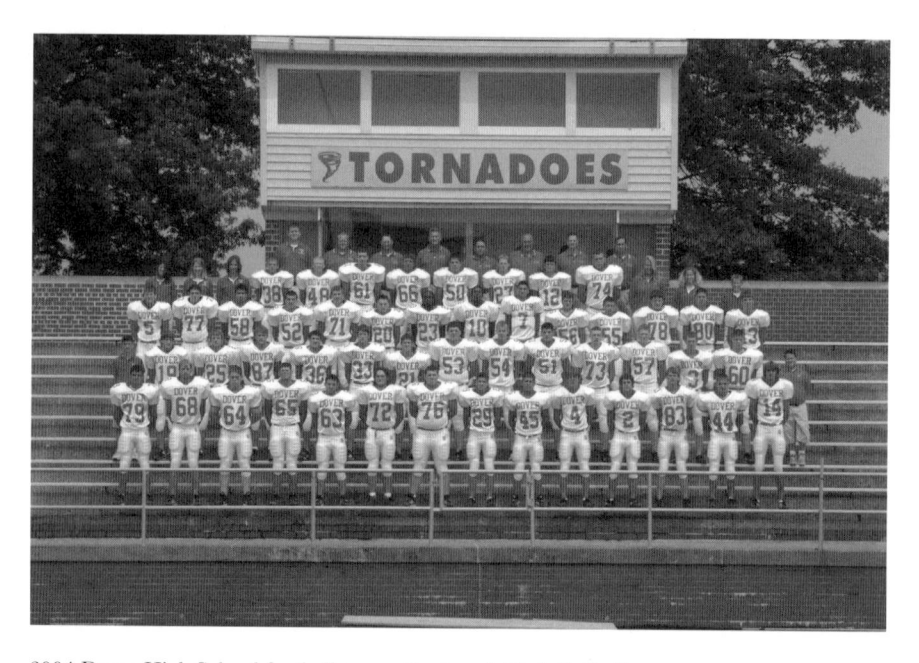

2004 Dover High School football team. *Courtesy of Mitchell's Studio.*

The Modern Era

New Philadelphia coach Matt Dennison. *Courtesy of Mitchell's Studio.*

of the ECOL championship and a spot in the state football playoffs. Led by second-year coach Matt Dennison, the Quakers featured a powerful offensive line that averaged 250 pounds per man. The main beneficiary of this talented line was senior running back Chad Franklin. Coming into the Dover game, Franklin sat at 1,280 yards for the season. A good game against the Tornadoes would give him the Quakers' all-time single season rushing record. In addition to his rushing yards, Franklin had also scored eighteen touchdowns in the Quakers' first nine games.

Also contributing to the Quaker offense that averaged 42.3 points per game was quarterback Alex Meiser. For the season, Meiser had completed 51 of his 110 pass attempts for over one thousand yards and fourteen touchdowns. Meiser's leading receiver was junior Richard Sandilands with nearly six hundred yards receiving and eight touchdowns.

Complementing the New Phila offense was a stout defense led by linebackers Corey Swinderman and Mark Sexton. For the season, opponents averaged only seven points per game against the Quakers.

Looking to test the tough New Phila defense was Dover's run-and-gun offense led by sophomore quarterback Daniel Ifft. Ifft, the oldest son of Dover

The Dover-Phila Football Rivalry

coach Dan Ifft, had thrown for a remarkable 2,214 yards in just nine games. In addition to the yards, Ifft's arm had produced twenty-seven touchdowns as Dover averaged a whopping 43.2 points per game. The leading receiver for the Tornadoes in 2004 was Corey Colaner, who had forty-nine catches and ten touchdowns. Dover was definitely a pass-first offense, as its leading rusher on the year was quarterback Daniel Ifft, with only 337 yards.

The 100th renewal of the annual rivalry was played in front of a sell-out crowd at New Philadelphia's Quaker Stadium. Projections put attendance numbers somewhere in the neighborhood of eight to ten thousand, although this number is difficult to pinpoint as many fans crowded Wabash Hill for a glimpse of the action and thus weren't counted in the official figures.

Taking the opening kickoff, New Phila's offense immediately showed that it could move the ball on the Tornadoes. It drove all the way down to the Dover seven-yard line in ten plays but came up empty. Stopped on third down, the Quakers opted for a field goal, which sailed wide right.

Dover took over and proved that it, too, could move the ball. Putting together a fifteen-play drive, the Tornadoes took the ball all the way down to New Phila's twenty-five but also came up empty. Forced into a fourth and five, the Quaker defense stepped up, and Dover couldn't convert. These two early drives would set the tone for the game as both high-powered offenses were held to half their average outputs.

The first big play of the game came when Richard Sandilands, the eventual game MVP, intercepted a Daniel Ifft pass at the Dover forty-five-yard line. Feeding off the momentum from the turnover, New Phila drove all the way to the Dover twelve-yard line before disaster struck. Instead of a second quarter lead, the Quakers faced a deficit after a costly fumble was returned by the Tornado defense for the game's first score. On the play, the Dover defender, Cody Kaderly, scooped up the ball and rambled eighty-two yards for the touchdown.

Despite the surprise turn of events, the stunned Quakers quickly regained their poise. As Dover lined up to kick the extra point, Mitch Clark burst through to block the extra point attempt. With 8:36 left in the second quarter, Dover held a 6–0 lead. The lead would stand through halftime as both teams continued their bend-but-don't-break defensive play.

New Philadelphia would take the lead in the third quarter with a nine-play, forty-four-yard drive. The capper came on a seven-yard run by Chad

The Modern Era

Franklin. Franklin would go on to rush for 148 yards in the game. This was enough to give him the Quakers' single season rushing record as he finished the year with 1,435 yards.

New Phila kept rolling in the third quarter. After stopping Dover's offense, the Quaker special teams stepped up. Speedy Brandt Smith returned a Dover punt sixty-six yards to put the Quakers up by a score. A successful extra point followed, and Dover found itself down 14–6.

On the very next drive, the Tornado offense answered the challenge, driving seventy-six yards in seventeen plays. Unfortunately for the Tornadoes, it would all be for naught as a bobbled snap on fourth and goal at the one ended the drive. Although they weren't able to score, the drive pinned the Quakers deep and gave Dover good field position after New Phila was forced to punt. On that punt, Dover's Kohl Fach broke loose and scampered all the way down to the Quaker one. Daniel Ifft snuck in from there, and Dover had pulled within two. On the ensuing extra point try, Ifft found receiver Keene Marstrell wide open for the conversion, and the score was all knotted up at 14–14.

With the final seconds ticking away in the fourth quarter, Dover would get an opportunity to win the game and spoil the Quakers' perfect season. The scoring attempt was set up by an odd turn of events that gave Dover good field position. On the play, New Phila's punter inadvertently touched his knee down in scooping up a low snap. This gave Dover possession at the New Phila twenty-five with very little time remaining in the game.

Dover took over, and Ifft advanced the ball five yards on first down to take the offense to Phila's twenty. On the next play, Dover was pushed all the way back to the thirty-six after a holding penalty. As time ticked off, the Tornadoes had to come up big to get back into field goal range. They did just that as Ifft found receiver Kyle Tharp, who flipped the ball to Keene Marstrell for a nice gain, taking back the yardage the Tornadoes lost on the penalty. With only time for one more play, Dover lined up to attempt the game winner. Unfortunately for Tornado fans, it wasn't to be. The forty-two-yard attempt fell just short, and the 100th game became the first ever overtime contest between the two rivals.

According to overtime rules, both teams get a shot at the ball. New Phila took over first and didn't waste any time. On the first play of overtime, Alex Meiser found Richard Sandilands for a big gain all the way down to the one. On the very next play, Meiser snuck into the end zone for the go-ahead

THE DOVER-PHILA FOOTBALL RIVALRY

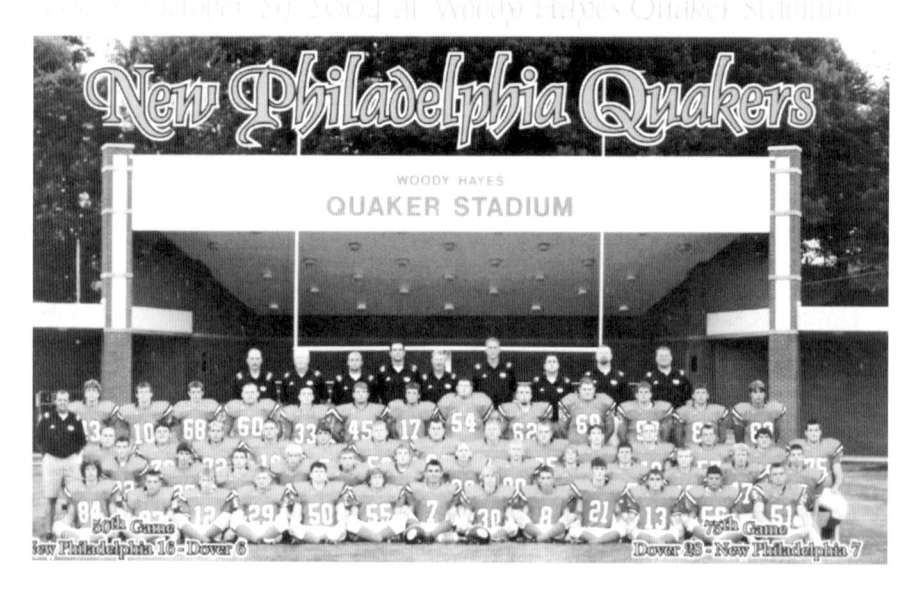

Program cover for the 100th Dover-Phila game. *Courtesy of the Tuscarawas County Historical Society.*

score. After a successful extra point, New Phila led 21–14, and it was Dover's turn to try and tie or win the contest.

Taking over at the twenty-yard line, the Dover drive almost identically mimicked the score by New Phila. Dover quarterback Daniel Ifft found

The Modern Era

Corey Colaner for eighteen yards before sneaking in from the two to make the score 21–20. The decision made by Dover's coach Dan Ifft on the extra point attempt provided one of the most exciting finishes ever to the big game. After Dover lined up in position to kick the extra point, New Phila called a timeout to ice kicker Kyle Tharp. It also wanted to ensure that it was prepared if Dover elected to try a fake. After the timeout, Dover again lined up to kick the extra point. On the attempt, the ball was snapped to Dover backup quarterback and holder Percy Garner, who flipped it to kicker Kyle Tharp. As the entire stadium held its breath, Tharp made a beeline for the right pylon. To the absolute delight of the Quaker faithful, New Phila defenders Richard Sandilands and Curt Urban corralled Tharp and brought him down at the two.

As the referee signaled the end of the game, the New Phila crowd exploded in a roar of jubilation. The perfect season was intact, and the nine-game losing streak was over. The gutsy call by the Dover coaching staff had come up just short. It was a fitting end to the 100th meeting of one of Ohio's oldest rivalries.

2005: NEW PHILA, 31; DOVER, 28

Coming into the 101st meeting with rival Dover, the New Phila Quakers were again on a roll. Coach Matt Dennison had the boys playing great. With only one game left on their schedule, the Quakers sat at 18-1 in their last nineteen games and had another opportunity to play for both a share of the conference title and a guaranteed home playoff game. The only thing that stood between them and one of the most successful stretches in New Phila football history was their old crosstown rival the Dover Tornadoes.

Despite all this success and the rebirth of New Phila football, the Quakers somehow found themselves the underdogs to a Dover team with a record of 7-2. Although their record was one win worse than the Quakers, this was a Dover team that had scheduled both Canal Fulton Northwest and the Massillon Tigers as its two non-conference games. Starting the year at 1-2, Dover then went on a roll, surging to six straight wins, all by double digits. The closest game the Tornadoes had been in since losing to Northwest was a 52–21 trouncing of Cambridge. It was probably this game more than any other that gave the "experts" their reasoning for picking the Tornadoes in the matchup. New Phila's only loss of the year came in heartbreaking fashion to Cambridge, 31–27.

Another factor that many saw as key to a Dover win was the unfortunate loss of Phila's starting quarterback in week nine. Alex Meiser was one of the recognized on-field leaders for the Quakers. The senior quarterback had amassed over 1,000 yards passing and a dozen touchdowns. Meiser had also run for 580 yards and six more scores. More impressive, though, was his record as a starter. Coming into the final game of his senior season, the quarterback had tasted defeat only once, putting together a career mark of 17-1 at the helm of Phila's offense. In a tragic turn of events, Meiser sprained an ankle in week nine and would not play against the Tornadoes. His replacement was sophomore Jordan Miller.

Leading the charge for the Quakers, in addition to Meiser, was senior and 2004 Dover-Phila game most valuable player, Richard Sandilands. Sandilands was one of those players who could singlehandedly change the outcome of a game. On the field for nearly every play, the Quaker star had a knack for being in the right place at the right time. Coming into the 2005 Dover-Phila matchup, the combination of Meiser to Sandilands was magical. Sandilands was New Phila's leading receiver, with forty-three catches for 740 yards and eleven touchdowns. New Phila's other big piece of the offensive puzzle was tailback Brandt Smith. For the season, Smith had rushed for over 1,000 yards, caught seventeen passes for another 184 yards and scored twelve touchdowns. Despite all this talent and their record, the Quakers were still considered the underdog. All the Quakers' accomplishments aside, the biggest reason for the underdog tag was the completely ridiculous numbers the Tornado offense had put up during the 2005 season.

Led by an outstanding quarterback and a trio of receivers, Dover's offensive run-and-gun attack would have made Steve Spurrier proud. In the first nine games of the year, first-year starter Percy Garner had annihilated all of Dover's passing records, throwing for 3,220 yards and thirty-four touchdowns. This meant that for the season, Garner was averaging 355 yards per game passing and nearly four touchdown throws per contest.

While Garner's numbers were amazing, he couldn't have put them up without his talented receiving crew. Garner's main target was Daniel Ifft, 2004's record-setting quarterback, with eighty-one catches for 1,376 yards

The Modern Era

and eighteen touchdowns. In addition to Ifft, Garner could throw to senior and leading scorer Keene Marstrell and fellow senior Kohl Fach.

With what promised to be an offensive shootout, the game also held the potential for ending a long drought for the New Phila Quakers. Phila had not beaten Dover at Crater Stadium since 1991 and had not won two in a row since the 1990 and 1991 seasons. To the surprise of no one, the game was again a sellout as the hometown crowd hoped for revenge for the heartbreaking loss in 2004.

As New Phila marched onto the field for its first series, it was led by sophomore Jordan Miller, as Meiser's ankle had left him less than 100 percent. The young sophomore quickly found his rhythm. He executed the playbook to perfection, driving the Quakers all the way into the home team's end zone. The young Miller must have learned a thing or two watching Meiser, as his primary target was none other than Richard Sandilands. With just over eight minutes left in the first, the two connected on a fifteen-yard fade, and the Quakers had a 6–0 lead. A successful extra point by kicker and soccer standout Ben Behrendt stretched the lead to 7–0.

Dover, as it had so many times in 2005, went about its work with a businessman-like approach. It put together a drive of its own to even the contest. Kohl Fach took the Quaker kickoff for fifty yards all the way down to the New Phila thirty-seven, where Garner took over. Dover's talented quarterback completed five passes to bring the Tornadoes to the two, where Keene Marstrell made the score 7–6 on a two-yard run. After a hiccup on the extra point, the score remained 7–6.

The score stayed the same through the rest of the first quarter and into the second when New Philadelphia got moving again. It drove all the way to the Dover eight before Sandilands and Miller hooked up again for another six. On the touchdown, Sandilands made a sliding grab over the right pylon for the Quaker score. Another successful extra point kick and the score stood at 14–6.

Much like on the first Quaker score, Dover again answered. Immediately following the Phila score, the Tornadoes put together a drive that culminated in a sixteen-yard pass from Garner to his favorite receiver, Daniel Ifft. The score, and the ensuing two-point conversion pass to Keene Marstrell, tied the game at 14–14. On its very next possession, after stopping the Quakers, the Dover offense took over and proved just how explosive it could be. With twenty-five seconds left in the half, the Tornadoes scored again. This time the touchdown came on a five-yard pass to Kolh Fach. Just like that, fourteen unanswered points had given Dover a 21–14 halftime lead.

Whether it was the halftime speech or the coaches' adjustments, the Quakers came out tough in the second half. With Dover receiving and with the opportunity to put the Quakers down by two scores, the Phila defense came up big. It stopped Dover's vaunted offense before taking the ball and showing the Tornadoes that this year's game would not be a Dover blowout. The scoring drive was a whopping fifteen plays for sixty-seven yards, eating up all of the three and a half minutes that remained in the third. The scoring play came, yet again, on a pass from Miller to Sandilands. This time, the play in question was a six-yard strike. The extra point was good, and with a little over three minutes left in the third, the game was even at 21–21.

Once again, as if answering the Phila challenge, the Dover offense went to work. Quarterback Percy Garner completed eight straight passes to take the Tornadoes inside the ten. From there, Keene Marstrell took over carrying the ball across the goal line to push Dover back in front, 28–21, setting up an exciting fourth quarter comeback.

After Dover faltered on its first possession of the fourth quarter, the Quakers took over and put together a masterful drive. It took ten plays to navigate the sixty-three yards to the end zone, with most of those yards coming on big plays. For once, the thorn in Dover's side was not Sandilands. Instead, Miller found tight end Doug Johnson for completions of twenty-four and twenty-two yards, respectively. These big plays set up tailback Brandt Smith, who toted the ball three consecutive times, scoring on third and goal from the three.

Unfortunately for the hometown fans, this time the Dover offense couldn't answer the Quaker score. After gaining only one first down, the Tornadoes were forced to punt, giving New Phila a chance to win the game. On what would become the game-winning drive, Miller connected twice with Sandilands and once with Jimmy Laner. The eighty-yard march also included tough running by Brandt Smith. Smith would end the game with 106 tough yards on twenty-seven carries. With only twenty-five ticks left on the clock, kicker Ben Behrendt trotted onto the field to attempt the game winner. With the ball placed at the one, Behrendt wrote his name in the history of the rivalry with a successful eighteen-yard game-winning field goal.

The Modern Era

Dover did get the ball back, but even the Tornado offense couldn't score with only twenty-five seconds left. The game ended when Sandilands intercepted a Percy Garner "Hail Mary" pass. It surprised no one that Richard Sandilands was there to make the pick. It also surprised no one when he was named MVP for a second consecutive year. In the game, the Quaker senior had nine catches for 132 yards and three scores.

While a great deal of the Quaker success was due to Sandilands, you can't forget the contribution of the young sophomore quarterback Jordan Miller. In the biggest game of his young career, the Quaker quarterback completed seventeen of twenty-eight passes for 234 yards and three touchdowns. More importantly, he protected the ball, throwing no interceptions in the contest.

Conclusion

Most young men who grow up in Dover or New Philadelphia do so dreaming of football greatness. It starts young as we all learn to root for our teams through spirit days, bonfires and pep rallies. That tradition continues as we first suit up for battle in one of the community's youth football programs. We learn the basics of the game and begin to pay a little more attention as our fathers tote us to the traditional Friday night games in Tuscarawas County.

It is about this time that those lucky enough and dedicated enough to persist in the sport begin to dream. The younger we are, the greater the dreams. For some of us, it's Joe Namath or Joe Montana leading the charge; for others, it's Tom Brady or Peyton Manning. What player we dream of being often changes from one year to the next. In the end, who we dream of being is not what is important. What is important is the greatness that the player represents and the accomplishments of the team.

As time passes and these young men grow, their dreams of greatness on Sunday afternoons begin to fade. Maybe some still dream of playing on Saturdays, but most come to understand that their careers as a football players will most likely end on a Friday night when they are only seventeen or eighteen years old. As life intervenes, and the dreams of football greatness beyond Tuscarawas County fade, we come to realize just how important the opportunity to be part of the Dover-Phila rivalry is.

Conclusion

Approximately 99 percent of the young men who play football at Dover or New Philadelphia will never play in front of a crowd larger or more passionate than the one they find on a crisp evening in late fall. For all of these young men, this is their moment. They are Joe Montana, Tom Brady, Barry Sanders. All the blood, sweat, tears and effort they have spent learning the game and honing their skills is paid back in one glorious night. That is what it means to play in the big game. That is why it's so special. It is our reward, our return on investment.

Personally, I was lucky enough to play in three Dover-Phila games. Twice I tasted victory, and once I felt the heartbreaking sense of loss that comes with losing the big game. In the end, though, as I look back, it wasn't so much about the outcome on the field as it was about the opportunity to be part of something bigger. Whether you grew up wanting to play for the Quakers or the Tornadoes, you grew up dreaming of that moment—that one brief second in time where the hopes, love and admiration of a community were placed squarely on your shoulders. This is the gift your community gives back to you in exchange for your efforts. Every boy in the game gets to have

The 1896 New Philadelphia High School football team. *Courtesy of the Quaker Foundation.*

Conclusion

that feeling he's dreamed of since his dad first handed him a football or took him to a game.

As the rivalry moves into its second century of play, I can only hope that not much changes. As long as the two communities continue to support their teams, those young men will continue to work hard and dream. In the end, these two components are why the game is so special and why we carry our memories of the rivalry throughout the rest of our lives.

DOVER-PHILA RIVALRY TIMELINE

1904	Grover Rosenberry is hired as Dover's first coach.
1905	C. Paul Townsend is named as New Philadelphia's first coach.
1906	The game is modernized by the Intercollegiate Athletic Association.
1916	Ed Heikes of Dover becomes the rivalry's first documented one-hundred-yard rusher.
1924	New Phila is referred to as the "Quakers" for the first time in the *Daily Reporter* (in October).
1924	Clyde Mathias rushes for 260 yards in a lopsided victory for the Quakers, 64–0.
1926	The *Daily Reporter* begins using the nickname Tornadoes, although the school will not officially adopt it until 1940.
1928	New Phila hosts its first bonfire.
1928	Quaker Stadium dedicated on September 29, 1928.
1929	Dover and New Phila both join the Ohio Big Ten Conference.
1931	Don Foutz's rushes for 232 yards in the Dover-Phila game.
1931	This year is the first game to be filmed and the first game with a public address system.

Dover-Phila Rivalry Timeline

1931–33	Dover's "Era of Champions": a state basketball championship, a 30-1 record in football and the National Championship for the band in 1933.
1937	The first game is played in the new Crater Stadium.
1938	Woody Hayes is hired as New Phila's head coach.
1940	Woody Hayes experiences his first loss to Dover in his final game coaching the Quakers.
1946	This year sees the first real act of vandalism prior to the big game. New Phila's crossbar is stolen and ends up on Dover's bonfire.
1947	The first ever night game in the series sees record attendance.
1947	C. William "Bill" Kidd is hired as New Philadelphia's head coach.
1949	The "Battle of the Bat" begins.
1950	This year is the first time the Dover-Phila game is broadcast by WJER.
1955	Joe Lowery scores three touchdowns in an upset win over New Phila.
1956	New Phila, 72; Dover, 0. Phila wins the most lopsided game in the rivalry's history.
1960s	Widespread vandalism begins involving both schools.
1960	Dover joins the Cardinal Conference.
1963	New Philadelphia joins the Cardinal Conference.
1971	Todd Miller rushes for 185 yards against New Phila.
1980	Woody Hayes returns to speak at Furbay Dinner.
1980	Brown's coach Sam Rutigliano attends the big game and players Todd Espenschied and Steve Berentz provide inspiration for their teams.
1981 and 1982	Mickey Mamarella shines against New Phila.
1984	New Phila High School is badly vandalized.
1991	Lou "the Toe" Groza is the featured speaker for the annual pre-game banquet.
1992	This year is the senior class's first ever win against New Phila. Underclassmen carry Dover to victory. Scott Blind kicks the game-winning field goal with thirty seconds left.

Dover-Phila Rivalry Timeline

1995	Dan Ifft is hired as Dover's head football coach.
1999	Dover wins Tuscarawas County's first state football playoff game.
2002	Special teams win the game for Dover at a muddy Quaker stadium.
2002–03	Todd Lisowski is named Dover-Phila MVP.
2004	New Philadelphia takes the 100th meeting of the two teams in an overtime thriller.
2004–2005	Richard Sandilands is named MVP for the Quakers in consecutive years.
2006	Dan Ifft passes Dick Haines to become Dover's all-time leader in wins as head coach.
2008	Dover tops New Phila twice to gain the series lead for the first time.

ABOUT THE AUTHOR

Matthew Lautzenheiser is a native of Dover, Ohio, and a 1995 graduate of Dover High School. His love of football began at the age of ten when he joined the Dover Pee Wee Football League. He would continue to play football for the next eleven years. While playing on Dover's varsity team in 1992, 1993 and 1994, he took part in three Dover-Phila rivalry games. As a sophomore in 1992, he was fortunate enough to play in one of the best Dover-Phila games in recent memory. It still ranks as one of his greatest memories of high school. In three rivalry games, he twice was on the victorious team and once felt the sting of defeat at the hands of the mighty Quakers.

After high school, Lautzenheiser attended Hiram College, where he continued his football career, lettering twice. In 1999, he graduated with a bachelor's degree in history from Hiram, and in 2002, he was awarded a master's degree, also in history, from the University of Akron. For the past ten years, he has worked in public history, first with the Western Reserve Historical Society as a historian and later as the director of the Dover Historical Society and J.E. Reeves Home. Lautzenheiser's return to Tuscarawas County has been rewarding both personally and professionally as it has given him the chance to work on great projects like this one and to give back to the community.

Lautzenheiser currently lives in Louisville, Ohio, with his wife, Kelly, and sons, Douglas and Benjamin. This is his second book.

Visit us at
www.historypress.net